PRAISE FOR *ROCK THE SAT*

Safety schools of the world, be afraid. Be very afraid.

—Joshua Neuman
editor-in-chief and publisher of *Heeb* magazine

Concentration and focus are key issues to successful learning, and music as a complement to the witty words of these 13 songs…guarantees learning. It's not only a great idea, but this is GOOD music, too!

—Carol Montparker
professional concert pianist and author of
A Pianist's Landscape

Teenagers are avid music listeners…*Rock the SAT* will provide a superb avenue to increase test scores.

—Ernest Taub
retired English chairperson and assistant principal
Northport High School, Northport, NY

Finally…a way to make the tedious, monotonous, and stressful process of developing an "SAT worthy" vocabulary fun and productive.

—Jane Burstein
high school English teacher and SAT tutor

Rock the SAT taps into the love of media and technology of today's teenagers.

—Mark F. Goldberg, Ph.D.
educational editor and consultant and author of
The Insider's Guide to School Leadership

With a rebel yell, the creators of *Rock the SAT* have grabbed the mic and shouted "Hell, no!" to all that, ripping the SAT lexicon from the clutches of the bland and giving it to the *band*.

—**Adam LeBow**
SAT tutor
Los Angeles, CA

Rock the SAT is incredibly impressive, delivering a relevant, age-appropriate, and accessible SAT study guide gift-wrapped for those nontraditional learners who better respond to alternative learning styles.

—**Robert J. Kaufman**
executive director, McAuliffe Regional Charter
Public School

A creative, valuable, and praiseworthy SAT study guide, enabling students to memorize important vocabulary simply by listening to catchy music.

—**Kathleen Smith**
English teacher, Oceanside High School
Oceanside, NY

Rock the SAT transforms the difficult task of learning new vocabulary into a creative, surprisingly enjoyable activity.

—**Shelly Auster, Ph.D.**
professor of English
Brooklyn Polytechnic University

The creators of *Rock the SAT* do what all good teachers do: they make learning enjoyable as well as meaningful.

—**John-Paul Spiro**
assistant professor of Humanities
Villanova University

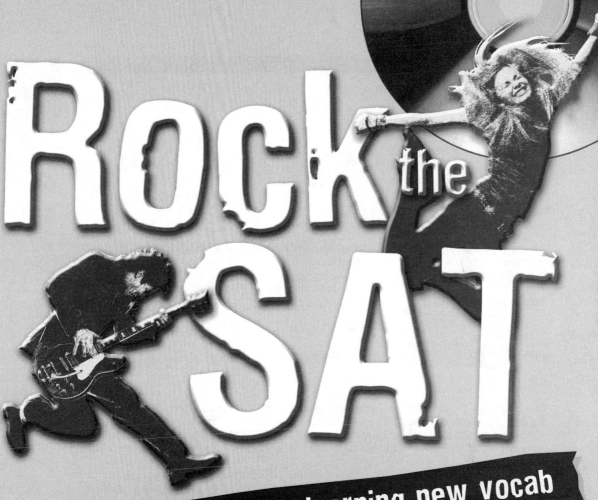

Rock the SAT

Trick your brain into learning new vocab while listening to slamming music!

MUSIC AND LYRICS BY
David Mendelsohn and Michael Moshan

TEXT BY
Michael Shapiro, Ph.D.

McGraw-Hill
New York   Chicago   San Francisco   Lisbon   London   Madrid   Mexico City   Milan
New Delhi   San Juan   Seoul   Singapore   Sydney   Toronto

The **McGraw·Hill** Companies

1 2 3 4 5 6 7 8 9 0 DOC/DOC 0 9 8 7 6

ISBN 0-07-146904-4
Part of
ISBN 0-07-146903-6

This publication is designed to provide accurate and authoritative information in regard to the subject matter covered. It is sold with the understanding that the publisher is not engaged in rendering legal, accounting, or other professional service. If legal advice or other expert assistance is required, the services of a competent professional person should be sought.

> —From a declaration of principles jointly adopted by a committee of the American Bar Association and a committee of publishers.

SAT is the registered trademark of the College Entrance Examination Board, which has not endorsed this publication.

The characters in this book are entirely fictional. Any similarities with persons living or deceased are entirely coincidental. The opinions of the characters as expressed in this book do not necessarily reflect the opinions of the authors.

McGraw-Hill books are available at special quantity discounts to use as premiums and sales promotions, or for use in corporate training programs. For more information, please write to the Director of Special Sales, Professional Publishing, McGraw-Hill, Two Penn Plaza, New York, NY 10121-2298. Or contact your local bookstore.

This book is printed on recycled, acid-free paper containing a minimum of 50% recycled, de-inked fiber.

Interior photographs by Jeffrey Cassuto.

CONTENTS

ACKNOWLEDGMENTS

Special thanks to the following people for their incredible support and steadfast belief in us and *Rock the SAT*. You guys truly rock.

Michael and Barbara Mendelsohn, Larry and Judith Moshan, Jeffrey Mendelsohn, Brook and Avi Gesser, Alex Smithline, Shana Liebman, Robert and Suzi Kaufman, Bob Reed, Mike Karp, Alana Fishberg and Daryl Kessler, David Wiesner, Jeff Fagen, Ze Frank, all the musicians who helped make the music sound slamming, Jacqui LeBow, Colin Mysliwiec, Karyn Rachtman, Jordan Birnbaum, Vikram Chiruvolu, Phil Padwe, Michael Blitzer, Dave Herman, Jeffrey Cassuto, Jon Feinstein, Lawrence Crimlis, Sheen Saleem, Gloria Miller, Ian Zeretsky, Harlan Silverstein, Eric Jacobson, Erik and Carri Weissberg, Swati, Liana Bergman, Risa Bergman, Marion Weil, Stuart Schwartz, Mitchell Epner, Lorin Shapiro, Doug LeBow, Julian and Christy Lowin, Mara Waldman, and Larrivee Guitars.

Also, much love and thanks to our amazing friends for being there with us every step of the way.

MUSIC NOTES

Music and lyrics by David Mendelsohn and Michael Moshan

Lead Vocals:	**David Mendelsohn**
Guitars:	**Bobby Lee Rodgers** **Ze Frank** **David Mendelsohn**
Keyboards:	**Tom Beaver**
Drums:	**Marco Giovino**
Bass:	**David Wiesner**
Backing Vocals:	**Jeff Mendelsohn, Jeff Fagen, David Mendelsohn**
Dobro on Imagination and Promontory:	**Tim Kelly**
Looping and Drum Programming:	**Jeff Fagen**
Recorded at:	**T-Street Studios, Boston** **Woolly Mammoth Studios, Boston**
Mixed at:	**Woolly Mammoth Studios, Boston**
Mastered at:	**The Toy Specialists, New York City**
Mastered by:	**Eric Jacobson**
Recorded by:	**Robbes Stieglitz, David Westner, David Wiesner, Tom Beaver**
Mixed by:	**David Wiesner, David Westner**
Produced by:	**David Wiesner**
Coproduced by:	**Jeff Fagen and David Mendelsohn**
Lyric Consultant:	**Michael Shapiro, Ph.D.**

Wake Up and Smell the Music!

Read This

You're pretty bright. You know what's up. You know the SAT isn't worth its weight in paper. You know it's not a reliable measure of your intelligence, and it certainly says nothing about your sparkling personality, dazzling good looks, and unparalleled good taste in music. It's racist, sexist, biased, and uses an ugly font. Its creators in sunny Princeton, New Jersey, are living high on the hog off the ridiculous fees you pay them in return for three hours of abuse on a Saturday morning.

You know the SAT is a hoop you jump through, like the good, trained dogs they want you to be. But this—this may be the mother of all hoops. How you perform on this test can, for better or worse, make all the difference in whether you win a Nobel Prize or spend the rest of your days eating cold cabbage soup in a train yard. If it comes down to the wire in the admissions office at Harvard, who are they gonna choose? The kid with the higher SAT score. (Yeah, cheerleading squad comes in a close second.) Because you want to go to college, you jump. Good dog. We jumped too, and we remember the pressure and pain. That's why we wrote *Rock the SAT*.

Some SAT prep companies can show you the ins and outs of the exam and how the test creators distract you from the right answers in all kinds of sneaky ways. Those courses can help you out, but even if you know every trick in the book, you won't score well if you don't know the vocabulary. It's just that simple. Can we emphasize that enough? Let's say it again, with feeling:

You Won't Score Well If You Don't Know the Vocabulary

Memorizing vocab is possibly the most boring endeavor known to humankind. Currently, there's no painless way to learn new words. You can drill endlessly from note cards or faithfully read the *New York Times* every day until the morning before your exam. Even then, you'll probably forget half of the words you tried to learn. *Rock the SAT* is our solution to this problem. Who knows, these words may even come in handy once the test is over. Or not. At a minimum, you can always impress people at parties or astonish your parents' friends when you lob, "Excuse my impertinence, but I do hope you're not interpreting my ebullient nature as being supercilious" at them. Whether you're a slacker, a bookworm, or someone in between, *Rock the SAT* will help you memorize the vocab.

*R*ock the SAT is a collection of 13 songs. Each song uses approximately 20 vocabulary words commonly found on the SAT. Forty-five minutes of music later, you've got 264 vocabulary words that you can recall with the tap of your foot! You have no problem remembering the complete lyrics to TV commercial jingles you saw when you were six, rotating wildly on your Sit & Spin to get that awesome disorienting rush. Music has a way of finding your long-term memory centers and setting up shop. It's probably the best method around for remembering just about anything.

Why these 264 words? We scoured recent SAT exams and a plethora (a lot) of study guides to find the most frequently tested words.

What is Rock the SAT?

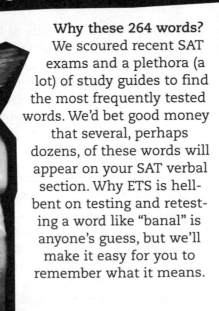

Why these 264 words?
We scoured recent SAT exams and a plethora (a lot) of study guides to find the most frequently tested words. We'd bet good money that several, perhaps dozens, of these words will appear on your SAT verbal section. Why ETS is hell-bent on testing and retesting a word like "banal" is anyone's guess, but we'll make it easy for you to remember what it means.

Who wrote the songs?
The songs in *Rock the* SAT are real tunes. In other words, they're not just jingly, nursery rhyme-type tunes designed specifically to help you memorize. They were not written by uptight vocabulary geeks working full-time for some mega-SAT study guide supercenter. They were written by the two musical geniuses on our team, David Mendelsohn and Michael Moshan, who live, write tunes, and perform in downtown Manhattan. David and Michael are hip, brooding, poor and, to hear them tell it, wickedly sexy studs who also happen to have very large vocabularies with which they fail to impress women. They wrote these tunes to be catchy, edgy, and slamming, using their massive talent for good instead of evil to produce

what we feel is the best and most painless program around to help boost your scores on the SAT verbal.

These songs are not just lists of words; we've used the words in context so that their meanings are, if not completely obvious, easy to figure out. In some cases, you might not know the exact definition of a vocabulary word in the lyrics, but having some familiarity with it will give you an enormous advantage over the kid sitting next to you who hasn't got a clue and is dripping sweatballs all over his or her bubble sheet.

What's with the workbook?

Just in case the songs aren't enough for your comfort and sense of well-being, we've also included this handy workbook with the CD. Our vocabulary guru, Dr. Michael Shapiro, is an English professor by day and, well, an English professor by night also. In the book, here's what he does with each word:

- defines it simply.
- uses it in a hilarious sentence.
- supports it with synonyms, antonyms and, when necessary, a few notes about how the word is used.

We've also included exercises to reinforce your understanding and memorization. It's important to use the CD with the workbook. Here's why:

- The music will give you the edge in memorizing.
- The sentences will show you the words in action.
- The exercises will help you get comfortable using the words in a testing situation.

We also strongly recommend that you read the lyrics while listening to the music, especially the first few times you listen. This will not only help you understand the lyrics, it will also give visual support to what you're hearing.

Rock the SAT is pretty focused. We want to help you achieve better SAT verbal scores by learning crucial vocabulary. We mostly steer clear of other stuff like test-taking strategies because you can get that elsewhere. Remember, this is a supplement to other preparation you choose to do, and it's a great cramming tool. What we want you to do is listen to the music until you've learned the words and then

Rock this test!

The SAT should not stand between you and four years of serious, mind-bending study at the college or university of your choice. Listen to the songs again and again and again; it will be impossible not to remember them. Do that and your score will rise. It's inevitable. Incipient. Imminent. Unavoidable. Predestined. Inescapable. Impending. It's just bound ta' happen.

Good luck,

YOUR BROTHERS IN ARMS,

Michael, David and Michael

We've set up each chapter for maximum ease and comfort. We're taking a "get in, learn the stuff, get out" approach. Remember, everything you read and hear in *Rock the SAT* is designed for one purpose and one purpose only: to help you memorize crucial vocabulary.

Workbook Chapters

The Words

We've divided the chapters into bite-sized, easy-to-swallow sections with each song getting its own chapter:

- Each chapter begins with the lyrics to the song. The vocabulary words appear in bold type.

- We then give you each vocabulary word with its part of speech (noun, adjective, verb, or adverb) and its definition.

- The vocabulary word is then used in a funny and memorable sentence. Some of these words have more meanings than we list, but we give you the meaning(s) most likely to appear on the test.

- We give you a couple of synonyms (words that mean the same) and antonyms (words that mean the opposite) to make life even easier. All synonyms and antonyms in bold type are SAT words you'll find elsewhere in *Rock the SAT*.

- Most of the words have a few notes about how to use them correctly. We also give you some fun facts—the word's etymology (history) or how to break it down into its prefix and suffix.

Exercises

Exercises? I thought you said *Rock the SAT* was different! It is different, but we would be selling you short if we didn't give you the chance to practice. We give you several types of exercises after each chapter to drill home the words.

Following the exercises is an answer key. For the sentence completions we explain why each answer is correct and why some answer choices, which seem like they ought to be right, are just plain wrong. Don't take it personally. There's no room for ego on standardized tests. Finally, to reinforce how the vocabulary and definitions are used in the tunes, we throw in the line of the song where the word appears and include that in the explanation. Lyrics appear in italics with the vocabulary and definitions both underlined, so you can pick 'em out easily.

Now go into your room, put in the CD, crank up the volume, and when your parents yell at you, tell them you're studying for the SAT!

A Note on Sentence Completions

Although *Rock the SAT* is all about the vocab, there are a couple of basic approaches to sentence completions that you should know about. Our explanations in the answer keys assume that you'll be trying to use these techniques as you work through the questions.

For sentence completions, follow these steps:

• Read the sentence (but don't read the answer choices yet!).

• Think of your own word to fill in the blank(s).

Once you think you've got a decent possibility, look through the answer choices and find the word that seems closest to the one you thought of.

If you have trouble, look for the "keyword," a word or phrase in the sentence (often another vocabulary word) that gives you a strong clue about what type of word or idea should appear in the blank. For example:

a. hiding
b. regenerating
c. hunting
d. hibernating
e. breeding

1. During the winter, bears will sleep for months; by _____ they can conserve their energy when food is scarce.

First, fill in the blank with your own word. The keywords are "sleep for months." This phrase tells you what must go in the blank. Choice d is, therefore, the best choice because that's what *hibernating* means. *Hiding* sounds like it could work, but it doesn't mean sleeping.

Use this technique for all your sentence completions. If you know the vocabulary, you'll rock.

How to Use Rock the SAT – 13 Steps to Glory

- 🎵 Put the *Rock the SAT* CD in your stereo and crank it. Loud. When the police knock, ignore them.

- 🎵 Listen to a couple of tunes—don't try to swallow the whole thing at once.

- 🎵 IMPORTANT: Read the lyrics as you listen.

- 🎵 Listen to the tunes again.

- 🎵 And again.

- 🎵 And again.

- 🎵 If the spirit moves you, feel free to sing along.

- 🎵 Read the definitions of the words and the sentences. Hysterical laughter encouraged.

- 🎵 Eat something unhealthy. Like a hot dog. Or paste.

- 🎵 Listen to the tunes again, and then test yourself. Can you sing the lyrics? Can you define *banal*?

- 🎵 When you think you're on the ball, try the exercises that go with the tunes.

- 🎵 Do this with all the tunes, and keep listening to the CD.

- 🎵 Go kick some SAT butt!

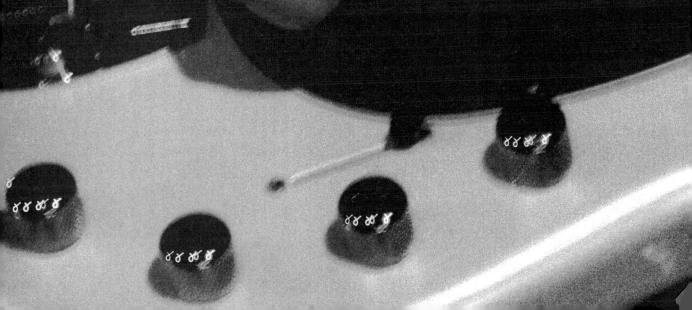

SILENCE, RETICENCE

Silence, Reticence

You're so **impertinent**
You're so **impudent**
You talk back all of the time
Stupefied
It dulls my senses
It numbs my state of mind
Where does that get me now
A weak, **futile** voice in the crowd

Silence, **reticence**
Be **taciturn**
Strive to be **laconic** to the point
Where you don't speak
You and me communicate
Strictly by **telepathy**
Don't speak

You act **belligerent**
Savage and **truculent**
Why must you fight with me
Don't you know
You're just a **charlatan**
You're not what you pretend to be
Where does that get you now
Vilified, abused, **denounced** by the
   crowd

Silence, **reticence**
Be **taciturn**
Strive to be **laconic** to the point
Where you don't speak
You and me communicate
Strictly by **telepathy**
Don't speak

Be **serene**
Peaceful to the extreme
Embrace **tranquility**
Embrace **tranquility**

I'm just a **novice**
A **neophyte**
I'm a beginner, this is all so new
Let me be
Your **sanctuary**
Let me shelter you

Silence, **reticence**
Speak easy
Be **taciturn**
Strive to be **laconic** to the point
Where you don't speak
You and me communicate
Strictly by **telepathy**
Don't speak
Don't speak...

Impertinent [*adjective*]

DEFINITION 1: rude or overly bold

As your superior officer, I will not tolerate any **impertinent** behavior from you warty, pimple-pocked maggots. You're a disgrace to the Girl Scout uniform.

SYNONYMS: insolent, **impudent**
ANTONYMS: polite, respectful

DEFINITION 2: irrelevant

These new facts about an impending asteroid strike are **impertinent** to my investigation of who's been using my toothbrush.

SYNONYMS: unrelated, unimportant
ANTONYMS: pertinent, relevant

Notes Don't get thrown by the fact that the word *pert* appears in the middle of *impertinent*. *Pert* means "overly confident," or "cocky." It can also mean "lively." Although it **sounds** as though *impertinent* could be a negation of *pert*, it's really a negation of the word *pertain*, which means "to relate to."

Impudent [*adjective*]

DEFINITION: offensively bold

When the **impudent** student mouthed off for the eighth time, Mrs. Gimmelstob briefly fantasized about quitting her job and running off with Ghoukas, an Armenian goatherd she met at the track.

SYNONYMS: insolent, **impertinent**
ANTONYMS: respectful, courteous

Notes Usually, *impudence* is what we call it when the person being disrespectful is younger or in a lower position of authority. A teacher can't, for example, behave *impudently* toward a student (though they can be jerks). Think of the word *imp* in the first syllable: a small, troublemaking demon known for mischief but which is no real threat.

Stupefied [*verb or adjective*]

DEFINITION: past tense of *stupefy*, to stun or make stupid

Alan **stupefied** Jeanne-Marie by admitting that he was dating her only to get closer to Nippy, her lovely Yorkshire Terrier.

SYNONYMS: astonished, dumbfounded
ANTONYM: unsurprised

Notes To *stupefy* is literally to shock someone to such a degree that they become stupid—unable to either talk or react intelligently. This word has an indirect relationship with *stupendous*, which means "really big." If something is *stupendous*, it's so big or overwhelming that it *stupefies* the viewer.

Something *stupefying* can inspire a sense of wonder or beauty in addition to simple shock. It tastes great as an adverb, too, especially when you want to insult someone as in: "That was a *stupefyingly* ignorant remark."

Futile [*adjective*]

DEFINITION: producing no result

When Marvin's efforts to find a prom date proved **futile**, he made one out of duct tape, latex, and his mother's wig.

SYNONYMS: fruitless, vain
ANTONYMS: fruitful, rewarding

Notes *Futile* is rarely used to mean "**frivolous**," as when one gets distracted by things of no consequence. Still, the primary meanings of "pointless," "useless," and "fruitless" are the most likely to appear on your test. Hence the utter *futility* of our forcing you to read about the alternative meaning, which is also, by the way, totally *impertinent*.

Reticence [*noun*]

DEFINITION: hesitancy to speak or act

Ingmar's **reticence** about his love for Elsie was a mistake; if only he'd spoken up, he might not have spent the last 15 years single, lonely, and listening to Light FM.

SYNONYMS: **taciturnity**, restraint
ANTONYM: outspokenness

Notes *Reticence* is most often used to mean "unwillingness to speak." This can be for whatever reason: people were sworn to secrecy; they're scared of sounding stupid by opening their fat mouths; or they're just tired and want to quit jawing all the time. Whenever people resist speech, they're *reticent*.

It can also mean "an unwillingness to act," as in: "I'm *reticent* about sending in the last of the army; all I've got left are the Fifth Infantry Elite Sewing Corps. And I believe they're already busy stitching 'We Won!' on my boxers."

Taciturn [*adjective*]

DEFINITION: using few words, soft-spoken

Because he was so **taciturn**, Joey did not call out for help while a swarm of rabid gerbils devoured his little sister.

SYNONYMS: **reticent**, uncommunicative
ANTONYM: **garrulous**

Notes Something *tacit* is unspoken: "We had a *tacit* agreement: though we never said it aloud, we all knew that if one of us got busted, we'd sell the others up the river to avoid jail time." *Taciturn*, therefore, means "disinclined to speak."

When people are described as *taciturn*, it can mean that they characteristically express themselves with few words. "Even in death, dad was pretty *taciturn*: his last words were simply: 'Buh-Bye.'"

Strive [*verb*]

DEFINITION 1: to exert a great deal of effort

Strive for greatness and work hard to achieve your goals. If that doesn't work, cheat and lie.

SYNONYMS: labor, toil
ANTONYMS: give up, be lazy

DEFINITION 2: struggle, fight against

After a lifetime spent at sea, **striving** against hurricanes, pirates, and bouts of scurvy, I've come to realize I hate sailing.

SYNONYMS: contend, vie
ANTONYM: be at peace

Notes Be on the lookout for the noun form, *strife*, meaning "struggle," "conflict," or "turmoil": "Decades of *strife* had so exhausted the Buttkikians that they shelved their plans for world domination and took a nice long nap instead."

Laconic [*adjective*]

DEFINITION: brief and to-the-point

Laconic by nature, Alfred needed only one sentence to alienate his friends, family, and an entire religious sect.

SYNONYMS: terse, succinct
ANTONYMS: **verbose**, rambling

Notes   This word comes from Laconia, a region of ancient Greece where the city-state of Sparta was located. Warlike and brutish, the Spartans weren't renowned for their communication skills; they preferred to negotiate with the talking end of a spear.

Telepathy [*noun*]

DEFINITION: the ability to read another's thoughts or to communicate by thinking

Using my powers of **telepathy**, I'm getting strong vibes that either you want me to be your macho hunk of all-American manhood or you're craving a cheeseburger.

SYNONYM: mind-reading

Notes   *Telepaths* are those who really *can* read another's thoughts—those who just *say* they can are called something else: *charlatans* (see page 10).

The suffix -*pathy* means "emotion." *Tele*- means "far" (that's why they call it *tele*-vision). Then it's easy to put together: *telepathy* is "far-feeling."

Belligerent [*adjective*]

DEFINITION: hostile and warlike

In an attempt to change its image as a **belligerent**, warlike nation, Germany is offering free bratwurst and sponge baths to the Czechs.

SYNONYMS: **bellicose**, violent
ANTONYMS: peaceful, nonviolent

Notes For this one, as well as *bellicose* (see "Amazing"), the prefix is the key. *Belli-* means "war," which you'll sometimes see used in political science or history books as *antebellum* (before the war) or *casus belli* (cause of war).

Truculent [*adjective*]

DEFINITION: brutal and savage

After another devastating defeat, Jets fans had grown so **truculent** that Security Guard Johnston, forced to control the violence, dusted off his cattle prod, crooning "Now's our chance, my pet."

SYNONYMS: fierce, barbaric
ANTONYMS: calm, sedate

Notes Don't get suckered: this word has nothing to do with trucks. It comes from the Latin *trux*, a word used to describe the savages who, to the Romans, included pretty much anybody who wasn't a Roman.

Charlatan [*noun*]

DEFINITION: a con artist or fake

When Abner tried to sell bottles of his sweat, claiming its scent would attract the opposite sex, most folks suspected he was a **charlatan**. Grandpa ordered 60 bottles anyway, just in case it was true.

SYNONYMS: fraud, quack

> **Notes** We got this word in a pretty roundabout way: although it sounds French, it was originally Italian, *ciarla*, meaning "to babble or chatter." Some speculate that the word was intended to suggest the quacking of ducks—from which it was an easy step to *ciarlatano*, a quack.

Vilified [*verb*]

DEFINITION: past tense of *vilify*, to speak badly about a person or thing

Because Gandhi resisted the British Empire's rule in India, the British **vilified** him, cursed his name, and wouldn't give him any kidney pie at tea.

SYNONYMS: defamed, reviled
ANTONYMS: commended, **lauded**

> **Notes** *Vilification* is no casual expression of dislike. If you **really** hate something, you *vilify* it. That's why it sounds so much like *vile*, which is about as nasty a four-letter word as you can use in the English language without getting kicked out of class.
>
> If you get stuck on this one, remember *evil* or *devil*, two things worth *vilifying*.

Denounced [*verb*]

DEFINITION: past tense of *denounce*, to speak badly about or publicly accuse

Although the member states of the United Nations loudly **denounced** the tyrant Boris Popopovich's unspeakable acts of oppression, they quietly accepted the millions of barrels of cheap oil he pumped into their economies.

SYNONYMS: defamed, blamed
ANTONYMS: **extolled**, praised

Notes Anytime you –*nounce*, you're saying something out loud. That's where we get *announce, renounce,* and *pronounce.* To *de-nounce*, then, is to say something negative out loud.

The noun form, *denunciation,* shows clearly where the word came from: *nuntius* is Latin for "messenger" or "speaker."

Serene [*adjective*]

DEFINITION: quiet, peaceful

Simone became **serene** when she realized it was only Saturday; she still had two days to prepare her speech to Congress, which would surely bring the nation to its knees.

SYNONYMS: **tranquil**, sedate
ANTONYMS: agitated, troubled

Notes What a lovely, calming word. Don't you feel the *serenity* when you say it out loud?

Tranquility [*noun*]

DEFINITION: peace and quiet

The **tranquility** of the Smith family reunion was shattered when cousin Ernest released his pet cobra into the kiddie pool to distract the others away from the sweet, sweet fruitcake.

SYNONYMS: calm, **serenity**
ANTONYMS: turmoil, chaos

Notes There's a reason why they call them *tranquilizers*. Take enough of them and you'll be mellow for hours, drifting sleepily in front of the television in a blissful haze of peaceful mindlessness. Not that we would ever encourage such a thing: everyone knows television rots the brain.

Remember that the word shares a root with *trance*, which suggests a peaceful (though sort of disconnected) mind state.

You'll sometimes see the word spelled with one l, sometimes with two. Both are correct. Just depends on how lazy you feel.

Novice [*noun or adjective*]

DEFINITION: a beginner

As a **novice** poet, Arthur wrote himself into a corner when he tried to find a rhyme for the line, "Thou art succulent as an orange."

SYNONYMS: **neophyte**, amateur
ANTONYMS: ace, skilled

Notes The Romans gave us so much, like the concept of bathing regularly. Back in ancient times, this was a pretty novel idea, since everybody was used to their apelike stench. *Novus*, the Latin word meaning "new," gives us both *novel* and the word at hand, *novice*.

People can be *novices* when they're just starting out, but things can also be *novice* if they're designed for use by a beginner, as in a *novice* ski slope.

Though our *novice* poet in the above sentence is both new *and* bad, the word *novice* does not necessarily imply badness. Only newness.

Neophyte [*noun*]

DEFINITION: a beginner

Neophyte skiers should never try the expert slopes; those mangled lumps scattered along the tree line were once human beings like you, with thoughts and feelings and absolutely no idea how to turn.

SYNONYMS: **novice**, tyro
ANTONYMS: expert, pro

Notes Ain't it good to know you've got so many ways to say a simple thing? *Neophyte* and *novice* are exact synonyms. Which one you choose says a lot about you and about how many friends you're likely to have.

Sanctuary [*noun*]

DEFINITION: a place of refuge or safety

Thank heavens a **sanctuary** has been created to protect the world's least attractive mollusk, the poisonous, flesh-eating slime sucker.

SYNONYMS: haven, shelter

Notes A *sanctuary* can be a physical place or a state of being. It's often used to describe a place, like a church or temple, that is protected because it is considered holy. Another common meaning is "a protected natural area," such as a *wildlife sanctuary*.

LYRIC FREAKS!

Directions: Fill in the blanks with a word (or words) from the lyrics.

1. Don't you know

   You're just a _____

   You're not what you pretend to be

   a. novice
   b. sanctuary
   c. charlatan
   d. neophyte
   e. telepath

2. I'm just _____

   _____

   I'm a beginner, this is all so new

   a. belligerent—Truculent
   b. impertinent—Impudent
   c. a novice—A neophyte
   d. vilified—A charlatan
   e. sanctuary—Tranquility

3. Where does that get you now

   _____, abused, denounced by
   the crowd

   a. Reticent
   b. Truculent
   c. Laconic
   d. Belligerent
   e. Vilified

4. Be serene

   _____

   a. Savage, violent, and mean
   b. Tidy and clean
   c. Invisible, unseen
   d. Peaceful to the extreme
   e. Jump around and scream

5. You're so impertinent

   You're so impudent

   You _____ all of the time

   a. flip out
   b. backtrack
   c. talk back
   d. talk smack
   e. speak easy

PLUG IN!

Directions: Draw lines to match each word (or words) on the left to the correct definition on the right.

1. Impertinent, Impudent

2. Stupefied

3. Futile

4. Reticence

5. Strive

6. Laconic

7. Telepathy

8. Belligerent

9. Truculent

10. Charlatan

11. Vilified, Denounced

12. Serene

13. Tranquility

14. Novice, Neophyte

15. Sanctuary

a. Producing no result, fruitless, weak

b. Hesitancy to speak or act

c. To exert a great deal of effort

d. Overly bold

e. Hostile and warlike

f. Pretender, con artist, fake

g. Peaceful

h. Peace and quiet

i. Savage and brutal

j. Communication through thought

k. Stunned, Numbed

l. Verbally abused

m. Shelter, a place of safety

n. Brief and to-the-point

o. Beginner

16

AMP IT UP!

Directions: Fill in the blanks, choosing the word (or words) that best completes the meaning of the sentence.

1. The _____ of nations in conflict can be a serious threat to the peacetime stability of neighboring countries.

a. tranquility
b. belligerence
c. impudence
d. futility
e. reticence

2. We were _____ to suggest that we all leave the beach when everyone was clearly enjoying the _____.

a. impertinent—day
b. laconic—mirage
c. reticent—tranquility
d. serene—sojourn
e. compelled—sanctuary

3. Having just learned to fly, Elizabeth was still a(n) _____, although she had no problems handling a small plane.

a. telepath
b. charlatan
c. apprentice
d. novice
e. imp

4. If you don't _____ for greatness, you will always be average.

a. strive
b. desire
c. denounce
d. stupefy
e. opt

5. I should have guessed by his _____, one-word answers to my inquiries that this guy was a complete _____.

a. laconic—charlatan
b. terse—expert
c. futile—neophyte
d. thorough—intellectual
e. truculent—recluse

ANSWER KEY

Lyric Freaks!

1) c; 2) c; 3) e; 4) d; 5) c

Plug In!

1) d; 2) k; 3) a; 4) b; 5) c; 6) n; 7) j;
8) e; 9) i; 10) f; 11) l; 12) g; 13) h;
14) o; 15) m

Amp It Up!

1. b

Here we need a word that implies *disagreement* because of the keyword *conflict*. Although *impudence* seems like a possible choice, it doesn't necessarily lead to conflict, certainly not the kind of conflict that could lead to a widespread war. *Belligerence* is the only choice (*You're so belligerent/Savage and truculent/Why must you fight with me*).

2. c

We're faced with a choice between two possible answers, a and c. Although choice a makes sense and some might think it's rude or *impertinent* to suggest leaving the beach when everyone's having fun, nothing in the sentence indicates that. It's not as good as choice c, because if everyone were enjoying the beach, one would definitely be *reticent* to suggest leaving.

3. d

Why *novice* and not *apprentice*? Aren't they synonyms? Well, almost. An apprentice is someone who is being taught by a master in a given profession. Elizabeth might be an apprentice to a more experienced pilot, but the sentence only indicates that she's a beginner, so we've got to go with *novice* (*I'm just a novice, a neophyte/I'm a beginner, this is all so new*).

4. a

Although several answer choices might seem to fit, only one is the best answer. *Desire* is not as good as *strive* because striving for greatness makes you more likely to achieve it than simply desiring it. *Opt*, which means "choose," is wrong because you can't just choose to be great. Wouldn't it be great if you could?

5. a

First, you have to find a word that means "quiet" or "terse" because of the "one-word answers." That eliminates everything but choices a and b. From there, a *charlatan* would be more likely to give short answers to cover up his or her lack of knowledge, while an *expert* would be more likely to expand on a topic (*Don't you know/You're just a charlatan/You're not what you pretend to be*). Therefore, choice a is your best bet.

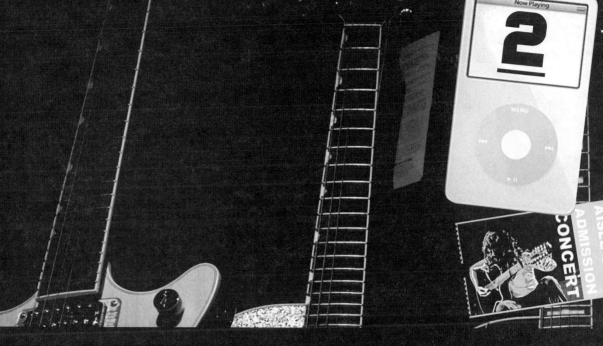

Now Playing

2

MENU

AISLE ADMISSION

CONCERT

HARBINGER

Harbinger

You're a **harbinger** of good things to come
A sign that it's all changing for me
It's happiness, **euphoria**, it's something out of a fantasy

Life was so **jejune** before I met you
It was so ordinary
Prosaic and **banal**, **pedestrian**, **mundane**
Nothing extraordinary
So I took a **sojourn**, I took a short trip
I needed a **respite**
A break from the routine that **enveloped** me, that surrounded me

Well I look back with **incredulity**
I cannot believe that you rescued me

You're a **harbinger** of good things to come
A sign that it's all changing for me
It's happiness, **euphoria**, it's something out of a fantasy
I'm so **morose** when you're not around
I'm sad and glum when I'm all alone
I've a **penchant** for your company
Your company is my tendency
We're balanced, you and me
We are **symmetry**

Let me be a **raconteur**, a storyteller
Tell you my **agenda**
A list of ways for us to celebrate, to **exult** in each other

Turn our love into a wild fire, a **conflagration**, burning through
  and through
Turn our love into a **mosaic**
A picture with a million different pieces spelling out the words
  "I love you"

When I saw you I had an **epiphany**
A **revelation**, a moment of clarity

You're a **harbinger** of good things to come
A sign that it's all changing for me
It's happiness, **euphoria**, it's something out of a fantasy
I'm so **morose** when you're not around
I'm sad and glum when I'm all alone
I've a **penchant** for your company
Your company is my tendency

You're a **harbinger** of good things to come
A sign that it's all changing for me
It's happiness, **euphoria**, it's something out of a fantasy
I'm so **morose** when you're not around
I'm sad and glum when I'm all alone
I've a **penchant** for your company
Your company is my tendency
You're the state of being supreme
You are **supremacy**
We're balanced you and me
We are **symmetry**
Yeah you're the state of being supreme
You know, you must be **supremacy**
You're my little **harbinger**, you're my little **harbinger**
A sign that things are gonna change...

Harbinger [*noun or verb*]

as noun

DEFINITION: an omen, a sign of future events

Just as the robin is a **harbinger** of the coming spring, so does that horrible mothball odor foretell the arrival of Grandma.

SYNONYMS: precursor, forerunner

as verb

DEFINITION: foretell

That horrible mothball odor **harbingers** the arrival of Grandma.

SYNONYM: predict

Notes Weird one, huh? It comes from a Middle French word, *herberge*, which meant a "hostel, inn, or lodge" (where we also get the word *harbor*). Back in the day, when people traveled in groups they'd send someone ahead to secure rooms in a *herberge* for the night. The person who was sent ahead to foretell the arrival of the group became our word for forerunner, *harbinger*.

Euphoria [*noun*]

DEFINITION: extreme happiness

Egbert felt absolute **euphoria** when Leslie let him borrow her red finger-paint, but his joy soured when he discovered that she had poisoned the paint with a powerful neurotoxin.

SYNONYMS: elation, **ebullience**
ANTONYMS: despair, **melancholy**

Notes Occasionally you'll see the adjective form, *euphoric*.

Jejune [*adjective*]

DEFINITION: boring, uninteresting

Marcus's observations about whether Captain Kirk is better than Captain Picard struck *Star Trek* fans as **jejune** because, after endless Internet chats, it had already been concluded that Kirk was a big, fat doofus.

SYNONYMS: **insipid, tedious**
ANTONYMS: exciting, original

Notes Another strange bird. It comes from Latin *jejunus*, meaning "empty of food" or "hungry." Now it's come to mean something that is devoid of value, that cannot sustain our interest and leaves us intellectually "hungry."

Prosaic [*adjective*]

DEFINITION: common, ordinary

I won't bore you with the **prosaic** details of my weekend-long marathon chess tournament against myself, except to say: I won.

SYNONYMS: **jejune, banal**

Notes You might recognize this word as the adjective form of the word *prose*. If you were paying attention in English class, you know that *prose* is the "opposite" of poetry. So, anything *prosaic* is said to be dull and flavorless, like the writing in your math textbook, while that which is poetic is interesting, unusual, and creative, like your favorite dirty limerick.

Banal [adjective]

DEFINIITON: lacking originality

Instead of releasing something new and interesting, Hollywood force-feeds us an endless stream of **banal** action movies in which muscle-bound goons blow things up.

SYNONYMS: **mundane, insipid**
ANTONYMS: fresh, original

Notes The noun form, *banality*, is less common but might be lurking around the corner somewhere.

Pronounce it *ba-NAL* or *BAY-nal* (depending on how snooty you want to sound).

Pedestrian [adjective or noun]

DEFINITION: common, uninteresting

Like many cheese snobs, Damien finds Swiss cheese too **pedestrian** for fine dining, and uses it instead as a deodorant stick.

SYNONYMS: **jejune, banal**
ANTONYMS: interesting, imaginative

Notes Almost everyone knows that the noun form of *pedestrian* means "a person traveling on foot," so it's unlikely you'll see it that much on the SAT. But it's important to remember it, because the ETS folk, who are devious indeed, might try to distract you with an incorrect answer that relates to walking.

Mundane [adjective]

DEFINITION: ordinary, commonplace

The fact that there are so many synonyms for **mundane** is a clear sign that we all need to turn off the TV and go out for some fresh air.

SYNONYMS: **banal, prosaic**
ANTONYMS: extraordinary, unusual

Notes The noun form, *mundanity*, may rear its ugly head occasionally: "Life is filled with the day-to-day *mundanity* of getting up, going to school, doing your homework, and pretending to care."

Sojourn [noun or verb]

DEFINITION: a temporary stay

After endless mineral baths, massages, and kelp wraps during her month-long **sojourn** at the spa, Dana was so relaxed she had to fly home in a bucket.

SYNONYMS: visit, break

Notes As a verb, to *sojourn* means "to stay temporarily."

Respite [noun]

DEFINITION: a brief rest

Between sets, the death-metal band Satan's Kitten went backstage for a relaxing **respite** and a nice bowl of matzoh-ball soup.

SYNONYMS: stay, reprieve

Enveloped [*verb*]

DEFINITION: enclosed completely

Hmmm. Death by slow-acting poison or death by being completely **enveloped** in a cloud of flesh-burning gas. That's a tough one; isn't there a death by chocolate option?

SYNONYMS: encircled, surrounded

Notes No problem with this one; just think of an *envelope*, which completely encloses whatever's inside it.

Incredulity [*noun*]

DEFINITION: disbelief

Stunned into disbelief, Cissy expressed her **incredulity** by shuffling in circles around the kitchen, mumbling over and over, "There's no such thing as a freezer goblin."

SYNONYMS: astonishment, **stupefaction**
ANTONYMS: **gullibility**, credulity

Notes You can remember this one easily enough by its similarity to *incredible*, which does not in fact mean anything like its slang meanings "awesome" or "amazing." It means "not believable."

An *incredulous* person is someone who's skeptical or disbelieving. However, be careful: a *credulous* person is not the exact opposite. It describes someone who believes things too easily.

Morose [*adjective*]

DEFINITION: gloomy or depressed

We all felt sorry for Richie when he was diagnosed with an illness that would slowly reduce him to a puddle of ooze, but after months of his **morose** depression, everyone secretly wished the disease would just finish him.

SYNONYMS: glum, **melancholy**
ANTONYM: cheerful

Notes We love all those gloomy words that begin with the prefix *mor-*, which is Latin for "death." Another great one is *morbid*, an adjective describing an overly gruesome, dark, or unwholesome interest in things, as in a "*morbid* fascination with hideous flesh sores."

Penchant [*noun*]

DEFINITION: a tendency or strong desire

Taylor's **penchant** for high explosives will either earn him a job on a demolition crew or turn him into tiny little bite-sized chunks.

SYNONYMS: affinity, inclination
ANTONYMS: dislike, aversion

Notes One always has a *penchant* for something: a *penchant* for chocolate cake or a *penchant* for the study of slime molds.

Symmetry [*noun*]

DEFINITION: an arrangement of balanced or harmonious proportions

While Buford's life was indeed tragic—he was born on a pig farm and died choking on a sausage link—it had a certain poetic, porkly **symmetry** to it.

SYNONYMS: equilibrium, proportion
ANTONYM: asymmetry

Notes The adjective form, *symmetrical,* or its antonym, *asymmetrical,* are equally likely to show up on your SAT.

Symmetry is not absolute; there can be degrees. If something is completely equal in all proportions, like a mirror image, then we might call it *perfect symmetry* or *absolute symmetry.*

Raconteur [*noun*]

DEFINITION: a person who excels at telling stories

Always a witty **raconteur**, Tijan captivated his audience with tales of his adventures in Malaysia, where he wrestled with the rare and fearsome speckled newt.

SYNONYM: storyteller

Agenda [*noun*]

DEFINITION: a list of things to do

Undergoing surgery wasn't on today's **agenda**, but since my legs have been severed from my body, I guess I'll add it to the list.

SYNONYMS: plan, schedule

Notes You might get a little thrown by the word's use in a common phrase, *hidden agenda,* which suggests some kind of dark, secret plot. By itself, the word *agenda* is neither positive nor negative; it's simply a plan or a list.

Exult [*verb*]

DEFINITION: to express extreme joy

The British soccer fans **exulted** in their team's victory by trampling each other in a mad rush to the field.

SYNONYMS: rejoice, celebrate
ANTONYMS: **lament**, mourn

Notes   The noun form, *exultation*, meaning "a celebration" or "expression of joy," is also fair game on the SAT: "The Italian and Portuguese fans were more than happy to join in the *exultations* by helping to trample the British soccer fans."

Be careful of this word's very close similarity to *exalt*, which means "to glorify" or "to elevate." It can appear in several forms, such as the noun *exaltation* and the adjective *exalted*: "The *exalted* Lord Huffingspout was once, like you, lowly as a smelly commoner."

Conflagration [*noun*]

DEFINITION: a disastrous or uncontrolled fire

The firemen could not contain the unbelievable **conflagration** caused by little Sarah's Easy-Bake oven.

SYNONYMS: wildfire, blaze

Notes   To qualify as a *conflagration*, a fire has to be big, nasty, and dangerous. Bonus points if it's also wildly out of control.

Mosaic [*noun*]

DEFINITION: an image composed of many small, colored tiles or pieces

I'm making you a **mosaic** out of Sweet-Tarts for Valentine's Day, but I can't find the right color to represent the joyless agony that is the destiny of all humanity.

Notes   *Mosaics* were a popular art form in ancient Greece and Rome, often decorating the floors of rich people's homes. They were made of small tiles called *tesserae*. Today, any image composed of many smaller individual elements could be considered a *mosaic*, such as when you see a composite image of hundreds of tiny photographs arranged according to their colors.

Epiphany [*noun*]

DEFINITION: a sudden clarity or insight

After hours of memorizing vocabulary from note cards, Rajesh had a powerful **epiphany** and realized he was going about it all wrong. Inspired, he paid someone else to take his exam.

SYNONYMS: **revelation**, realization

Notes   An *epiphany* is usually something **really BIG**—in some cases, life-changing. Often it's applied to religious or spiritual experiences, or moments when you grasp some fundamental or essential truth. All *epiphanies* are sudden; one minute you're watching your cat fail to operate the electric can opener, the next you understand that God has a really cruel sense of humor.

Revelation [*noun*]

an astonishing discovery

Zookeeper McElroy conveniently disappeared when **revelations** about his peculiar fondness for licking toads came to light.

SYNONYMS: **epiphany**, realization

Notes   Often *revelations* are spiritual, as though a kind of divine communication occurs (hence one of the books of the Bible is called *Revelations*). A *revelation* can be less significant than that, but it is usually shocking or unexpected, sometimes pleasantly so, and sometimes, as in the case of our toad-licking zookeeper, quite the opposite.

Revelation is *not* the noun form of the verb *revel*, which means "to celebrate joyously."

Supremacy [*noun*]

the state of being the highest or greatest

Now that Alicia had achieved academic **supremacy** over her third-grade classmates, she set her sights on a higher goal: wrenching the student council vice-presidency from the iron fist of Stacey Feldman.

SYNONYMS: ascendancy, preeminence
ANTONYMS: inferiority, lowliness

LYRIC FREAKS!

Directions: Fill in the blanks with a word (or words) from the lyrics.

1. Well I look back with incredulity

   I _____ that you rescued me

   a. will not forget
   b. cannot believe
   c. believe in my heart
   d. sweetly recall
   e. always assumed

2. You're a _____ of good things to come

   A sign that it's all changing for me

   a. raconteur
   b. mosaic
   c. sojourn
   d. revelation
   e. harbinger

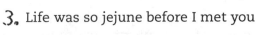

3. Life was so jejune before I met you

   It was so _____

   a. exciting
   b. perplexing
   c. ordinary
   d. terrible
   e. unappealing

4. So I took a(n) _____

   I took a short trip, I needed a _____

   A break from the routine

   a. respite–sojourn
   b. penchant–conflagration
   c. mosaic–harbinger
   d. epiphany–revelation
   e. sojourn–respite

5. Turn our love into a _____

   A picture with a million different pieces spelling out the words "I love you"

   a. conflagration
   b. harbinger
   c. revelation
   d. respite
   e. mosaic

PLUG IN!

Directions: Draw lines to match each word (or words) on the left to the correct definition on the right.

1. Harbinger
2. Euphoria
3. Jejune, Prosaic, Banal, Pedestrian, Mundane
4. Sojourn
5. Respite
6. Enveloped
7. Incredulity
8. Morose
9. Penchant
10. Symmetry
11. Raconteur
12. Agenda
13. Exult
14. Conflagration
15. Mosaic
16. Epiphany, Revelation
17. Supremacy

a. Celebrate, express extreme joy
b. Sign of things to come
c. Brief rest, a break
d. Tendency or strong desire
e. Image composed of many small pieces
f. Ordinary, common, uninteresting
g. Disbelief
h. State of being the highest or greatest
i. Extreme happiness
j. Sudden clarity or insight
k. Fire raging out of control
l. Balance, harmony
m. Surrounded, enclosed completely
n. Storyteller
o. Sad, glum, gloomy, depressed
p. Short trip
q. List of things to do

AMP IT UP!

Directions: Fill in the blanks, choosing the word (or words) that best completes the meaning of the sentence.

1. Always an entertaining _____, Jennifer's father told us many interesting stories about the time he went on safari in Africa.

   a. interviewer
   b. revelation
   c. raconteur
   d. poet
   e. journalist

2. I'm so bored by Barry's _____ insights about the benefits of Cream of Wheat over oatmeal; he just can't help being _____.

   a. prosaic–banal
   b. jejune–morose
   c. pedestrian–slow
   d. mundane–wordy
   e. annoying–foolish

3. Although I have a strong _____ for reading long novels, I decided to try something shorter this time, just for variety.

   a. ability
   b. penchant
   c. memory
   d. agenda
   e. sojourn

4. It is said that balance and _____ between the left and right halves of the face give the appearance of beauty.

   a. supremacy
   b. euphoria
   c. conceit
   d. integrity
   e. symmetry

5. The ancient texts recently discovered by the archeologists are a true _____ because they will uncover fascinating truths about the Ming dynasty.

   a. conflagration
   b. harbinger
   c. revelation
   d. respite
   e. mosaic

Answer Key

Lyric Freaks!

1)b; 2) e; 3) c; 4) e; 5) e

Plug In!

1) b; 2) i; 3) f; 4) p; 5) c; 6) m; 7) g;
8) o; 9) d; 10) l; 11) n; 12) q; 13) a;
14) k; 15) e; 16) j; 17) h

Amp It Up!

1. c

What makes this one tricky is that all the answer choices except choice b *could* be correct. The best answer, however, should be synonymous with the keyword *stories*; that word would be *raconteur* (*Let me be a <u>raconteur</u>, a <u>storyteller</u>*).

2. a

In the first blank you need a word that means "boring" because our speaker is bored by Barry. Oops. That means every answer choice except choice e could reasonably fit. We also know that the second word must mean something similar to the first, because Barry can't help being boring. That eliminates everything but choice a.

3. b

We know this person usually reads long novels, so we can reject choices c, d, and e, which don't convey that sentiment. *Ability*, although it makes sense, doesn't fit as well as *penchant*, which means "tendency or desire" (*I've a <u>penchant</u> for your company/Your company is my <u>tendency</u>*).

4. e

In this case, the keyword is *balance*, a dead-on synonym for *symmetry* (*We're <u>balanced</u>, you and me/We are <u>symmetry</u>*). The other choices simply don't feed the bulldog.

5. c

The best choice is the one that suggests "new learning or insight," which is exactly what *revelation* means. Something here is being revealed by the ancient texts, so c is the best choice (*When I saw you I had an epiphany/A <u>revelation</u>, a <u>moment of clarity</u>*).

Now Playing

3

MENU

MONOTONY

AISLE ADMISSION CONCERT

Monotony

I feel so **sluggish**, I can't get out of bed
I want to **obliterate**, to erase the thoughts inside my
head
I can't move, I've got no **mobility**
Well it's an **enigma**, it's a mystery what's happening
to me

It's the same thing
Oh, **monotony**
Gets so **tedious**
I don't care, so call it **apathy**
Every day is all that happens
Every day is all that happens

The sky is dark and **ominous**
It's so **foreboding**, it's so **menacing**, so threatening
The future looks **desolate** from here
Like a **clairvoyant** I can see the future and it's a
wasteland from here

It's the same thing
Oh, **monotony**
Gets so **tedious**
It's average, boring **mediocrity**
Every day is all that happens
Every day is all that happens

And why am I so **indifferent**, why don't I care
How do I **mitigate** the damage, and make it less
    severe
How do I **rectify** it, to make things right
I can't get a handle on it tonight
Tonight

The days are **uniform**, they're all the same
All this **conformity**, this similarity drives me insane
Nothing will **ameliorate** or ease the hurt
It's all a **brouhaha**, it's chaos and I'm just about to
    burst

It's the same thing
Oh, **monotony**
Something's got to give
I'm **impervious**, nothing gets through to me
Every day is all that happens
Every day is all that happens
Every day is all that happens
Every day is all that happens

THE WORD ON THE WORDS

Sluggish [*adjective*]

DEFINITION: inactive or slow-moving

Gertie is so **sluggish**, she once lost a footrace to an actual slug.

SYNONYMS: lethargic, slothful
ANTONYMS: energetic, lively

Notes To be fair, the slug was a record-holder in its species class.

Obliterate [*verb*]

DEFINITION: to destroy completely

A peaceful nation once famous for its delicious kiwi smoothies, Wimponia quickly surrendered when its neighbor Buttkikia invaded and **obliterated** all its blenders. Now Wimponia is just famous for its kiwis.

SYNONYMS: efface, eradicate
ANTONYMS: create, build up

Notes Notice the suffix –*literate*. Sounds like *literature*. To *obliterate* also means "to erase completely," as though you were wiping the words off a blackboard. You've completely removed all traces of the words, thus, *ob-literating*.

Mobility [*noun*]

DEFINITION: the ability to move

After the accident, Becky lost **mobility** in her jaw and couldn't speak, much to the relief of her friends, lawyer, and conjoined twin.

SYNONYMS: motion, motility
ANTONYM: immobility

Notes The adjective form, *mobile,* is just as common: "When Becky's jaw was once again *mobile*, it never stopped moving, not even when she slept."

Enigma [*noun*]

DEFINITION: a mystery or puzzle

The *Mona Lisa*'s mysterious smile has been an **enigma** for centuries, but many believe it was because she was saying "cheese" for 10 straight hours.

SYNONYMS: secret, riddle

Notes People are sometimes described as *enigmatic* if they're hard to read or mysterious. "Walter sure is *enigmatic*; he wears black latex pants, keeps his sunglasses on at night, and answers only to the name Elizabeth McGarnigle."

Monotony [*noun*]

DEFINITION: dreary regularity or sameness

Though hiding Egbert's asthma inhaler had become another **monotony**-filled kindergarten activity for Leslie, she continued to do it again and again and again and again.

SYNONYM: **tedium**
ANTONYM: variety

Notes When someone speaks in a *monotone*, his or her voice is flat and unchanging, much like that of our old French teacher, Mr. Murphy, who never failed to put us to sleep with his droning *monotone*.

Tedious [*adjective*]

DEFINITION: long and tiresome

Although it was going to be boring and **tedious**, Bethany was determined to knit thousands of tiny mittens for every last one of her imaginary friends.

SYNONYMS: **monotonous**, dull
ANTONYMS: interesting, exciting

Notes The noun form, *tedium*, means "the condition of boredom": "I can't bear the *tedium* of sitting in a dentist's waiting room any longer! Just hand me the pliers!"

Activities, like knitting thousands of mittens, can be *tedious*, and people—like the guy who can't seem to stop talking about his boring life as an accounting consultant for a midsized insurance company in Topeka, Kansas—can also be considered extremely *tedious*.

Apathy [*noun*]

DEFINITION: lack of caring or emotion

I feel such complete **apathy** toward you, it's as if you don't even exist. By the way, have you mailed our wedding invitations yet?

SYNONYMS: **indifference**, unconcern
ANTONYMS: caring, interest

Notes Remember that the suffix *–pathy* means "emotion" (don't forget the other *–paths*: *sympathy*, *empathy*, and *telepathy*). The prefix *a–* means "none." Put simply, "no emotion" is *apathy*, and *apathetic* people just don't care.

Some people confuse the word *ambivalent* with *apathy*. *Ambivalent* means that you feel more than one way about something: "I'm *ambivalent* about going to the movies; I want to hang with my friends, but I don't want to waste another 10 bucks on a piece of Hollywood garbage." *Apathetic* means you don't feel anything at all: "I'm *apathetic* about the movies. Go, don't go, whatever."

Ominous [adjective]

DEFINITION: predicting evil or disaster

Confronted by the gunslinger's **ominous** stare at high noon, Deputy DuPree decided he should have gone into his brother Melvin's flower-arranging business after all.

SYNONYMS: forbidding, **foreboding**
ANTONYMS: hopeful, reassuring

Notes *Ominous derives from the word omen, which is a sign of the future. Ominous, though, always has the sense of menace or disaster.*

Menacing [adjective]

DEFINITION: threatening danger or harm

Grandma kept us out of her kitchen by warning us in her most **menacing** tone, "Get out or I'll gut ya and throw ya in the stew!"

SYNONYMS: sinister, threatening
ANTONYM: comforting

Foreboding [adjective or noun]

DEFINITION: expectation of misfortune

Keith felt a **foreboding** sense of doom as his teacher handed out the tests. While he was comfortable with basic arithmetic, he didn't know squat about quantum hyperdimensional metaphysics.

SYNONYMS: portending, **ominous**
ANTONYM: encouraging

Clairvoyant [*noun or adjective*]

DEFINITION: one who can see the future

I didn't take it as a good sign when the **clairvoyant** ran from the room retching in the middle of my palm reading.

SYNONYMS: fortune-teller, seer

Notes This interesting word derives from the French *clair* (clear) and *voir* (to see), thus "see clearly." It can be used to mean the supernatural ability to predict the future, but it can also describe someone who's unusually perceptive.

There are two noun forms, *clairvoyance*—the ability itself, and *clairvoyant*—the person who possesses it.

Clairvoyant is also the adjective form: "He has a *clairvoyant* ability to predict the stock market. Unfortunately, he can only seem to tell when it's tanking."

Desolate [*adjective*]

DEFINITION: barren, uninhabited

While the desert seems **desolate**, it is actually teeming with creatures, most of which are either fatally venomous or extremely icky.

SYNONYMS: deserted, sterile
ANTONYMS: verdant, fertile

Notes Places can be *desolate* if they're empty of life, but people can also be *desolate* when they're extremely lonely: "As the last man on Earth, Didier felt empty and *desolate*. On the other hand, he could walk around buck naked, which was a small consolation."

The noun form, *desolation*, is the perfect word for any condition of total sterility or barrenness, such as you find on a dead planet like Mars or the parking lot of a shopping mall at 4:00 am.

Remember that the word sounds a lot like *desert* (not *dessert*, which is what you eat after dinner), and it's a no-brainer.

Mediocrity [*noun*]

DEFINITION: the condition of being average

Desiree was neither quiet nor talkative. She could run sort of fast but not that fast. She was the picture of **mediocrity** in everything she did, including kickboxing, but since I always won, I didn't care.

SYNONYMS: ordinariness, generality
ANTONYMS: extraordinariness, superiority

Notes   Remember that *medium*, which shares a root with *mediocrity*, means "average" or "middle." It's not necessarily a bad thing to be *mediocre*, but, well, it ain't that great either.

Indifference [*noun*]

DEFINITION: lack of interest or concern

I feel complete **indifference** as to whether a Democrat or Republican is elected president. For all I care, we could elect a freakin' monkey. Yeah, that's right. Monkey.

SYNONYMS: unconcern, **apathy**
ANTONYMS: engagement, interest

Notes   *Indifferent* can mean "apathetic," as in the example above, but it can also mean "unbiased" or "impartial": "I'm *indifferent* about whether a man or woman should be my servant as both are equally capable of being walked all over."

Just remember: if you wouldn't treat one thing differently from another, you're treating them with *indifference*.

Mitigate [verb]

DEFINITION: to ease or relieve

Gwendolyn didn't want to hurt Vance, so she tried to **mitigate** the blow. "It's not you," she said. "It's me. I've never been attracted to short, ugly losers."

SYNONYMS: **assuage, ameliorate**
ANTONYMS: worsen, aggravate

Notes Something that *mitigates* is only a part of a solution. It relieves a problem, but doesn't completely resolve it.

You'll often come across it in the phrase *mitigating circumstances*: "Dimitri should have failed his oral presentation, but because of *mitigating circumstances* (he had lost a third of his brain in a freak turkey-carving accident), the teacher gave him a D-."

Rectify [verb]

DEFINITION: to correct a mistake

Because Crawford failed to **rectify** a small accounting error on his tax return, the government was somehow legally entitled to his car, house, and first-born son.

SYNONYMS: amend, remedy
ANTONYMS: err, blunder

Notes You've probably already noticed this word shares a root with *correct*. If you haven't, then you just did. Done and done.

Uniform [adjective or noun]

DEFINITION: characterized by sameness

Because our schools discourage individuality, they create legions of bleary-eyed, **uniform** zombies destined to slave away in highway rest stops and law offices across the nation.

SYNONYMS: homogenous, consistent
ANTONYMS: heterogeneous, diverse

Notes *Uni-* means "one," and *–form* means, well, "form." So, you get "one form." Could this get any easier?

Its meaning as a noun is very narrow: distinctive clothes that identify a particular group of people. They're called *uniforms* because every cop, firefighter, and convicted criminal in your town is dressed alike.

Conformity [noun]

DEFINITION 1: the quality of sameness

Admiral Greaseburger's policy of **conformity** results in all of its franchises being exactly the same, right down to the mold spores in the secret sauce.

SYNONYMS: homogeneity, similarity
ANTONYMS: variety, diversity

DEFINITION 2: staying within accepted bounds of behavior or thought

Because we live in a civilized society, **conformity** is expected from each of us: we mustn't grope strangers on the subway, steal from convenience stores, or pelt meter maids with ice-balls.

SYNONYMS: submission, compliance
ANTONYMS: rebellion, nonconformity

Notes People don't like to think of themselves as *conformists*; we all want to be individuals. But if all of us want the same thing, doesn't that make us *conformist*? Oy, it hurts the head.

Ameliorate [verb]

DEFINITION: to make better

Whenever my ego needs a boost, nothing **ameliorates** my insecurities better than hanging out with Phillip the squid-boy.

SYNONYMS: **mitigate**, relieve
ANTONYM: intensify

Notes Like *mitigate*, to *ameliorate* means to relieve but not completely cure a problem.

Brouhaha [noun]

DEFINITION: a noisy, chaotic situation

After LaMaz checked Kruschenko into the boards, the big Russian slashed LaMaz's neck with his stick. Their enraged teammates clashed at center ice in a **brouhaha** of punching, eye-gouging, and face-eating.

SYNONYMS: pandemonium, uproar

Notes This word's presence on the SAT shows the ETS can, in fact, have a sense of humor. Most of us can't say this word with a straight face.

Impervious [adjective]

DEFINITION: incapable of being penetrated

Archibald built an **impervious** fortress to keep out everyone except his most faithful knights, his trusted advisors, and the pizza delivery guy.

SYNONYMS: impermeable, inviolable
ANTONYMS: penetrable, permeable

Notes *Impervious* can be used to describe something physically resistant, like the fortress in the above sentence, or it can mean "emotionally or mentally unaffected," as in: "Calling me a pea-brained scuzz-bucket will have no effect on me; I'm *impervious* to your insults."

LYRIC FREAKS!

Directions: Fill in the blanks with a word (or words) from the lyrics.

1. The days are _____, they're all the same

  a. ominous
  b. sluggish
  c. impervious
  d. uniform
  e. desolate

2. How do I mitigate the damage, and _____

  a. make it go away
  b. make it free from hurt
  c. make it disappear
  d. make it less severe
  e. make it civilized

3. It's the same thing

  Oh, _____

  Gets so tedious

  a. apathy
  b. mobility
  c. monotony
  d. mediocrity
  e. conformity

4. And why am I so indifferent, why _____

  a. don't I see
  b. don't I think
  c. don't I care
  d. don't I smile
  e. don't I move

5. How do I _____ it, to make things right

  a. ameliorate
  b. rectify
  c. obliterate
  d. mitigate
  e. conform

PLUG IN!

Directions: Draw lines to match each word (or words) on the left to the correct definition on the right.

1. Sluggish   a. Threatening

2. Obliterate   b. The ability to move

3. Mobility   c. Lack of interest or caring

4. Enigma   d. One who can see the future

5. Monotony, Uniformity   e. To destroy completely

6. Tedious   f. The state of being average

7. Apathy, Indifference   g. Incapable of being penetrated

8. Ominous, Foreboding   h. Sameness, dreary regularity

9. Menacing   i. Describing a sense of coming misfortune or disaster

10. Clairvoyant   j. To make right, to correct

11. Desolate   k. Barren, uninhabited

12. Mediocrity   l. Boring and tiresome

13. Mitigate, Ameliorate   m. Chaotic situation

14. Rectify   n. Mystery or puzzle

15. Brouhaha   o. Ease or minimize damage

16. Impervious   p. Inactive or slow-moving

AMP IT UP!

Directions: Fill in the blanks, choosing the word (or words) that best completes the meaning of the sentence.

1. I don't care whether we stay or go; I'm completely _____.

a. mediocre
b. tedious
c. sluggish
d. indifferent
e. impervious

2. The dark clouds on the horizon looked _____ and seemed to predict disaster.

a. angry
b. desolate
c. frightening
d. clairvoyant
e. foreboding

3. The ancient writing proved to be too much of a(n) _____ to the young translator, who couldn't figure out the meaning behind the intricate symbols.

a. enigma
b. brouhaha
c. tedium
d. omen
e. monotony

4. Although we try to encourage students to be different and not _____, we do require some regularity and _____ in behavior.

a. mediocre–average
b. harmless–regulation
c. apathetic–indifference
d. conformist–uniformity
e. average–seriousness

5. This painkiller should help to _____ your headache.

a. obliterate
b. desolate
c. rectify
d. ameliorate
e. intensify

ANSWER KEY

Lyric Freaks!

1) d; 2) d; 3) c; 4) c; 5) b

Plug In!

1) p; 2) e; 3) b; 4) n; 5) h; 6) l; 7) c;
8) i; 9) a; 10) d; 11) k; 12) f; 13) o; 14)
j; 15) m; 16) g

Amp It Up!

1. d

The keywords in this sentence are *don't
care*. If you don't care, you're *indifferent*
(*And why am I so <u>indifferent</u>, why <u>don't</u> I
care*). Done.

2. e

This is one of those situations where all
the words seem to fit, but only one
choice fits best. In this case, it's
foreboding, because something that's
foreboding predicts doom or a negative
outcome (*It's so <u>foreboding</u>, it's so
menacing, so <u>threatening</u>*). The clouds may
seem *angry*, *desolate*, or *frightening*, but
that doesn't mean they predict
anything. *Clairvoyant* is tricky because it
has an element of prediction. However,
a clairvoyant only sees the future—
there is nothing necessarily negative or
threatening about the prediction (*Like a
<u>clairvoyant</u> I can <u>see the future</u> and it's a
wasteland from here*).

3. a

This one is tough if you don't know the
vocab. An *enigma* is a puzzle or a
mystery (*Well it's an <u>enigma</u>, it's a <u>mystery</u>
what's happening to me*), which is exactly
what our young translator is facing, as
indicated by the keywords *couldn't
figure out*.

4. d

The keywords *different* and *not* tell us
that the first blank means the opposite
of different. Which choices fit this
need? Only choices d and e. The second
blank must mean something similar to
regularity. *Seriousness* doesn't mean that
at all, but *uniformity* certainly does (*The
days are <u>uniform</u>, they're <u>all the same</u>*).

5. d

Be careful of absolutes on the SAT—to
say something completely erases a
headache, which is what *obliterate*
means, is probably too absolute (*I want
to <u>obliterate</u>, to <u>erase</u> the thoughts inside my
head*). *Rectify* is incorrect for the same
reason. But something that helps to
ease the pain, to *ameliorate* it, is just
what we're looking for (*Nothing will
<u>ameliorate</u> or <u>ease the hurt</u>*).

Now Playing

4

AISLE
ADMISSION
CONCERT

AMAZING

Amazing

Can you hear me when I call to you
Or are my cries **inaudible**
You make me believe that my dreams
    can come true
Even if they're **implausible**

And when I catch a glimpse of you
I can't be quiet or **subdued**
My boldness, my **audacity**
Proliferates, it grows rapidly

You're amazing
You **satiate** and you satisfy
You're amazing
You **placate** and you pacify
My love for you is **steadfast**,
    unchanging

Do you notice that I'm even alive
Or am I that **inconspicuous**
Don't **eschew** me, don't push me
    aside
I'm so harmless, **innocuous**

And though you can be **bellicose**
Warlike to your greatest foes

Even they would never disagree
Cause there's **unanimity**
I'm not lying, it's no **fallacy**
To put it briefly, yeah with **brevity**

You're amazing
You **satiate** and you satisfy
You're amazing
You **placate** and you pacify
My love for you is **immutable**,
    unchanging
You're amazing

Everything else is so **nugatory**, of no
    importance, so **frivolous**
Anything more would be
    superfluous, so unnecessary, so
    extraneous

You're amazing
You **placate** and you pacify
You're amazing
You **satiate**, yeah you satisfy
My love for you is **steadfast**,
    unchanging
You're amazing
Yeah, you're amazing
You're so amazing
You're amazing

THE **WORD** ON THE WORDS

Inaudible [adjective]

DEFINITION: too quiet to be heard

The speckle-bottomed hyena can perceive sounds that are **inaudible** to humans. On the other hand, the speckle-bottomed hyena rolls in its own filth.

SYNONYMS: silent, imperceptible
ANTONYMS: audible, loud

Implausible [adjective]

DEFINITION: not believable, highly unlikely

Because dogs are carnivorous and don't typically eat paper products, your excuse for not handing in your homework is highly **implausible**.

SYNONYMS: unbelievable, **dubious**
ANTONYMS: plausible, believable

Subdued [adjective or verb]

DEFINITION: quiet, calm

Because my blind date was quiet and **subdued** during dinner, I thought she didn't like me. I was later relieved to learn she'd been born without a tongue.

SYNONYMS: **tranquil**, restrained
ANTONYMS: agitated, energetic

Notes *Subdued* is often used to describe a person's manner or tone of voice, as in the sentence above. It can also be applied to situations. (A *subdued* party would be a pretty mellow event.)

As a verb, *subdue* means to calm down a person or to bring peace to a chaotic situation. It can also mean to defeat an enemy: "At last we have *subdued* the rebellion! Let's eat."

Audacity [noun]

DEFINITION: boldness, often in the face of authority

When the math teacher called on Albertina to solve the equation, she showed her **audacity** by screeching, "Make me, geekazoid!"

SYNONYMS: brazenness, **impudence**
ANTONYMS: timidity, shyness

Notes   Don't confuse *audacity* with words that sound like it, such as *audible*, *audio*, or *audience*. *Audacity* has very little to do with sound or listening.

It's also common to see it in adjective form, *audacious*: "Albertina's *audacious* assault on the math teacher was universally respected among her fellow first-graders."

Proliferate [verb]

DEFINITION: to grow in number

Poison ivy wouldn't be a problem if it didn't **proliferate** so rapidly. Why can't the fun plants, like blueberry bushes, reproduce in great numbers? I like blueberries.

SYNONYMS: reproduce, multiply
ANTONYMS: die off, decline

Notes   You'll also find this word in its noun form, *proliferation*: "Some say the *proliferation* of nuclear weapons is the biggest problem facing the world today. I say those losers who drive Hummers while the globe heats up are a close second."

Satiate [*verb*]

DEFINITION: to satisfy a desire, often for nourishment

When several helpings of meat loaf, an entire rump roast, and a side of steamed eels couldn't **satiate** Sigurd, she demanded a dessert of blood pudding and diet cola.

SYNONYMS: fill, satisfy
ANTONYMS: starve, do without

Notes You'll sometimes find the verb *sate* used interchangeably with *satiate*. They mean the same thing and can be used the same way. One of 'em just sounds smarter. Less often, you'll see the noun forms: *satiation*, or the most rare among them, *satiety*. Don't worry too much about that last one; only English professors get off on using it.

Though you'll probably see *satiate* most often associated with physical hunger, it can be applied to any kind of desire: physical, emotional, intellectual, etc.

Placate [*verb*]

DEFINITION: to soothe or settle

Nothing we said could **placate** Morris; he was enraged that someone had scribbled the words "Beware of Dog" on his forehead during nap time.

SYNONYMS: appease, mollify
ANTONYMS: anger, antagonize

Notes You might see the adjective form, *placatory*, used to describe something that tries to be calming: "In fact, our *placatory* tone had the opposite effect: it only further angered Morris, who justified the sign on his forehead by snarling and barking at us."

Steadfast [*adjective*]

DEFINITION: not subject to change

Although Natalie tries to be **steadfast** and disciplined about maintaining a healthy diet, she still gets weak in the knees for a sizzlin' slab of deep-fried hog fat.

SYNONYMS: strong, **resolute**
ANTONYMS: weak, wavering

Inconspicuous [*adjective*]

DEFINITION: hard to see, not noticeable

The enormous monitor lizard is usually **inconspicuous** because it blends perfectly with the bush; once it leaps for your throat, however, it's pretty hard to miss.

SYNONYMS: hidden, concealed
ANTONYMS: conspicuous, obvious

Eschew [*verb*]

DEFINITION: to avoid habitually

The other sophomores **eschewed** Darius, often cutting through the library to avoid him, because it was rumored that he hadn't showered since the summer of 2004.

SYNONYMS: shun, abstain from
ANTONYMS: seek out, pursue

Innocuous [*adjective*]

DEFINITION: harmless

Egbert thought Leslie was an **innocuous** little girl, but he learned the truth when during a kickball game she slid into second base, and tried to skewer him with her cleats.

SYNONYMS: benign, inoffensive
ANTONYMS: harmful, dangerous

Notes Don't get confused between this word and the noun *inoculation*, which is a shot you get to protect yourself from disease. If you get stuck, though, you can think of a related word like *innocent*, which has a similar sense of harmlessness.

Bellicose [*adjective*]

DEFINITION: warlike, aggressively violent

A peaceful nation famous for its delicious kiwi smoothies, Wimponia quickly surrendered when its **bellicose** neighbor Buttkikia invaded and stole its recipe, altering the course of fruit-drink history forever.

SYNONYMS: hostile, **belligerent**
ANTONYMS: peaceful, pacifist

Notes You might see this word in its noun form, *bellicosity*: "To protect Wimponia from Buttkikia's *bellicosity*, the United Nations sent in its multinational juice-keeping force."

Belligerent is a close synonym of *bellicose*. See "Silence, Reticence" for more info.

Unanimity [noun]

DEFINITION: agreement from all, complete unity

Because Mitzi rejected society's **unanimity** of opinion about the benefits of personal hygiene, she spent most of her time alone in an alley, picking lice out of her armpits.

SYNONYMS: accord, unison
ANTONYMS: discord, disagreement

Notes It's much more common to see the adjective form, *unanimous*: "Her friends were in *unanimous* agreement: they would kidnap Mitzi and spray her down with a high-pressure hose before letting her back in the sorority."

Related words can help you if you get stuck: *unity, union, unify.* Remember: the prefix *uni-* means "one."

Fallacy [noun]

DEFINITION 1: a false idea or argument, a lie

It's a **fallacy** to say that finders are keepers and losers are weepers, especially when what you find is a big, angry monkey.

SYNONYMS: mistake, error
ANTONYMS: truth, fact

DEFINITION 2: a deceptive appearance

The harmless appearance of the Serbian Fuzz Bunny is a **fallacy**; as it approaches, the seemingly sweet creature lunges forward, injects its prey with venom, and feasts on the victim's twitching body.

SYNONYMS: disguise, deceit

Notes The adjective form, *fallacious*, is also common: "The Serbian Fuzz Bunny's *fallacious* appearance is the reason for its incredible success; because it's often mistaken for a harmless rabbit, it lures unsuspecting children to their untimely ends."

Fallacies can be intentional lies or disguises, but they can also just be innocent errors of logic or fact.

Brevity [*noun*]

DEFINITION: briefness

Since my English teacher always says that **brevity** is a virtue, she'll be thrilled that I trimmed my 10-page research paper down to a lean three.

SYNONYMS: terseness, compactness
ANTONYMS: long-windedness, **verbosity**

Notes You can remember this word by the similarity it shares with *brief*, which is actually its adjective form.

Immutable [*adjective*]

DEFINITION: unchanging, stable

Years of research have proven an **immutable** truth: when you drop a cat from an aircraft, it will, upon impact, become an ex-cat.

SYNONYMS: permanent, absolute
ANTONYMS: changing, mutable

Notes You can remember this word by considering its relatives, *mutation* and *mutant*. A *mutation* is a change in form. When you add the *im-* prefix, it acts like a negative. *Mutable* is changing, *immutable* is unchanging.

Nugatory [*adjective*]

DEFINITION: of no importance

The school board ignored Principal Schatz's **nugatory** proposal; there simply wasn't a pressing need for 75 electric cattle prods.

SYNONYMS: trivial, **inconsequential**
ANTONYMS: important, significant

Notes No, this word has nothing to do with *nougat*, that weird creamy stuff at the center of a candy bar.

Frivolous [adjective]

DEFINITION: unimportant or lacking seriousness

That gold-plated nostril probe may have been a **frivolous** purchase, but if we ever see a patient with acute mucus blockage, we'll be ready in style!

SYNONYMS: trivial, silly
ANTONYMS: serious, important

Notes *Nugatory* and *frivolous* are almost exact synonyms, but there is a slight difference. *Frivolous* implies a kind of lightness or silliness. *Nugatory* describes something that's useless, pointless, or futile.

Superfluous [adjective]

DEFINITION: unnecessary or extravagant

Though Crispin won the spelling bee with a powerful rendition of "diaphanous," his "Wooohoooo!" and butt-wiggling were a **superfluous**, tacked-on finish to an otherwise flawless performance.

SYNONYMS: **extraneous**, needless
ANTONYMS: necessary, integral

Notes Break it down, cousin: the prefix *super-* means "on top of," or "in addition to." The suffix *–fluous* means just what it sounds like: *fluid*. So imagine a cup of water overflowing and spilling on the table. You don't need all that extra water; it is *superfluous*.

Extraneous [*adjective*]

DEFINITION 1: not belonging

The natives of Tongaluvalongabong, an isolated Pacific island, lived in their traditional way for centuries. The sudden appearance of iPods and plasma TVs seems to be the result of some **extraneous** influence.

SYNONYMS: alien, external
ANTONYMS: belonging to, fitting in

DEFINITION 2: not an important part, not essential

I've finished assembling your artificial hip—and in record time! I just hope these leftover parts are **extraneous**.

SYNONYMS: **superfluous**, irrelevant
ANTONYMS: vital, essential

Notes *Superfluous* and extraneous are very close synonyms. Again, there's a subtle difference. Something that's *superfluous* is just wasteful or in excess of what you need. *Extraneous*, on the other hand, suggests that something is unrelated. Think of it this way: *superfluous* is too much. *Extraneous* is totally irrelevant.

LYRIC FREAKS!

Directions: Fill in the blanks with a word (or words) from the lyrics.

1. You're amazing

   You _____ and you pacify

   a. satiate
   b. eschew
   c. proliferate
   d. placate
   e. subdue

2. Everything else is so _____, of
   no importance, so _____

   a. bellicose–frivolous
   b. immutable–steadfast
   c. nugatory–frivolous
   d. nugatory–steadfast
   e. satiate–steadfast

3. Can you hear me when I call to you

   Or are my cries _____

   a. steadfast
   b. conspicuous
   c. innocuous
   d. unanimous
   e. inaudible

4. Don't eschew me, don't _____

   a. leave me behind
   b. tell me those lies
   c. push me aside
   d. try and act kind
   e. throw me a line

5. And though you can be bellicose

   _____ to your greatest foes

   a. worrisome
   b. wary
   c. warlike
   d. kind
   e. resentful

66

PLUG IN!

Directions: Draw lines to match each word (or words) on the left to the correct definition on the right.

1. Inaudible
2. Implausible
3. Subdued
4. Audacity
5. Proliferate
6. Satiate
7. Placate
8. Steadfast
9. Inconspicuous
0. Eschew
1. Innocuous
2. Bellicose
3. Unanimity
4. Fallacy
5. Brevity
6. Immutable
7. Nugatory, Frivolous
8. Superfluous, Extraneous

a. Boldness
b. Satisfy
c. Unnoticeable
d. Grow rapidly
e. A lie
f. Harmless
g. Unnecessary, not belonging
h. Quiet
i. Avoid, cast aside
j. Warlike
k. Resistant to change
l. Too quiet to be heard
m. Unchanging
n. Agreement from all
o. Unimportant
p. Briefness
q. Pacify, soothe
r. Not believable

AMP IT UP!

Directions: Fill in the blanks, choosing the word (or words) that best completes the meaning of the sentence.

1. To learn about the natural world, biologists must attempt to see and hear things that are normally invisible or _____.

   a. inconspicuous
   b. inaudible
   c. subdued
   d. obvious
   e. minute

2. Roseanne was allergic to sugar, and took great pains to _____ it.

   a. acquire
   b. mix
   c. eschew
   d. negate
   e. sate

3. Your story is so _____ that no one will ever believe you!

   a. steadfast
   b. conspicuous
   c. innocuous
   d. unanimous
   e. implausible

4. Rats are _____ at an alarming rate; if something isn't done quickly, they'll be all over the city.

   a. proliferating
   b. growing
   c. eating
   d. socializing
   e. placating

5. When speaking publicly, you must stress the important points; avoid _____ details and speak with _____ so your audience remains interested.

   a. extraneous–unanimity
   b. unanimous–frivolity
   c. boring–bellicosity
   d. superfluous–brevity
   e. implausible–honesty

Answer Key

Lyric Freaks!

1) d; 2) c; 3) e; 4) c; 5) c

Plug In!

1) l; 2) r; 3) h; 4) a; 5) d; 6) b; 7) q;
8) k; 9) c; 10) i; 11) f; 12) j; 13) n;
14) e; 15) p; 16) m; 17) o; 18) g

Amp it Up!

1. b

If we can't see something, it's *invisible*,
just as if we can't hear something, it's
inaudible (*Can you hear me when I call to
you/Or are my cries inaudible*).
Inconspicuous is a close possibility, but
it's not specific enough. *Minute* means
"tiny," but we can still hear tiny things.

2. c

The best fit for this blank would be a
word that means "avoid." Therefore,
eschew is the best choice here (*Don't
eschew me, don't push me aside*). *Negate* is
the only other possibility, but it doesn't
really make sense. How can you negate
sugar? *Sate*, which is another form of
satiate, means "to satisfy" and doesn't
make sense in the blank.

3. e

This one's straightforward. You need a
word meaning "unbelievable." Now,
which one is it? But of course,
implausible.

4. a

The answers throw you two pretty
good-looking possibilities: *proliferating* or
growing. *Proliferate* has a slightly
different meaning than *grow*, however.
It means to grow in number, not
necessarily in size. Therefore, choice a is
the best answer.

5. d

Here we're looking for words that mean
"unimportant" and either "interest" or
"briefness." Choice a seems promising
because *extraneous* works, but then
unanimity doesn't make any sense.
Choice c is incorrect because, although
details may be *boring*, they might still be
important. Speaking with *honesty* is
always a virtue, but your audience
might still lose interest, so choice e is
out. Choice d is correct because
superfluous means "unimportant"
(*Anything more would be superfluous, so
unnecessary, so extraneous*), and *brevity*
means "briefness" (*To put it briefly, yeah
with brevity*).

DUPED AGAIN

Duped Again

She was **presumptuous**
She was bold to the point of rudeness
But there was always so much **subtlety**
I never noticed how she treated me

She never liked it when I was **superficial**
When I only scratched the surface
Loving her could be **unnerving**
She often made me nervous

She had a **wry** sense of humor, a dry sense of
    humor, a **wry** sense of humor
She had a **witty** personality, clever personality,
    witty personality
Long may she **reign**
Rule over me with supreme power
She could be **supercilious**, so **haughty**, she
    looked down on me
But I barely noticed that about her

I want to be **duped** again
I want to be fooled again
And I may have been **deluded** and misled
But I felt so safe inside her spider web
Inside her spider web

Sometimes she'd **provoke** me
She'd arouse me into action
She'd pick on me because of my views
I'd say I suffered **persecution**

She never liked it when I was a **sycophant**
When I tried to be an ass-kisser
I guess it was **unsound** and unhealthy
But I, I could not resist her

She had a **fluid** way about her, a flowing way
   about her, a **fluid** way about her
She had a **plethora** of talent, a whole lot of
   talent, a **plethora** of talent
Long may she **reign**
Rule over me with supreme power
She could be so **irascible**, so **querulous**, so
   irritable
But I barely noticed that about her, oh that
   about her

I want to be **duped** again
I want to be fooled again
And I may have been **deluded** and misled
But I felt so safe inside her spider web
Inside her spider web. . .

Presumptuous [adjective]

DEFINITION: excessively forward

US/French relations would be less tense if a **presumptuous** American diplomat hadn't demanded that the French delegate give him a foot massage during the United Nations' Christmas party.

SYNONYMS: **impudent, impertinent**
ANTONYMS: shy, unassuming

Notes The more common form of the word is the verb *presume*, meaning "to reach a conclusion without real evidence." *Presumptuous* people are therefore often considered rude because they act before they have all the facts and go beyond what's proper. Even when *presumptuous* people are right, they're still annoying.

Subtlety [noun]

DEFINITION: delicateness

The **subtlety** of Candace's delicate perfume was lost on Dickie, who was busy sniffing his armpits.

SYNONYMS: refinement, **elusiveness**
ANTONYMS: crudeness, obviousness

Notes Usually you'll see this word as an adjective, *subtle*, which has several meanings:

delicate (as in a *subtle* perfume, as in the example above)

difficult to perceive (as in a *subtle* message)

refined (as in a *subtle* taste in art)

highly skilled (as in a *subtle* craftsman)

acting secretly or in a hidden way (as in a *subtle* poison)

artfully sly (as in a *subtle* villain)

Of course, your best bet is to know all of them, but you can get by with just "delicate" and "difficult to perceive." The others are really variations of these two basic meanings.

Superficial [adjective]

DEFINITION: only on the surface

Concerned only with his hairstyle, the finish on his Lexus, and the size of his biceps, Aston is not only incredibly **superficial**, he probably doesn't even know what it means.

SYNONYMS: trivial, shallow
ANTONYMS: deep, meaningful

Notes The most common use of *superficial* is to describe someone who cares only about appearances and has no substance or depth. You might also see it used to describe something that's only on the surface of things, such as a *superficial wound* (it doesn't cut too deeply) or a *superficial resemblance* (where two things appear to be similar on the surface but differ on deeper levels).

Unnerving [adjective]

DEFINITION: causing nervousness or fear

We found it slightly **unnerving** when Dolores waved her knitting needles in the air, screaming, "Worship me, for I am your new god!"

SYNONYMS: upsetting, frightening
ANTONYMS: calming, relaxing

Notes Don't get this word confused with another, similar sounding SAT word: *enervating*, which means exhausting or tiring. See "Frugal with Your Love" for more fun-filled information on this word.

Wry [*adjective*]

`DEFINITION 1:` cleverly and often ironically funny

Although Lester's sense of humor is usually **wry**, last night he somehow couldn't resist those "What's grosser than gross?" jokes.

SYNONYMS: dry, **witty**
ANTONYMS: crude, vulgar (as in humor)

`DEFINITION 2:` bent or twisted

That sewage pipe is set at a **wry** angle. If we don't straighten it out—and quick—very, very ugly things will happen to us.

SYNONYMS: crooked, askew
ANTONYMS: straight, correct

`Notes` You might come across a similar word, *awry*, which means pretty much the same thing as the second definition of *wry*, "bent or crooked." *Awry* can also be used when everything goes wrong: "All our carefully laid plans have gone *awry*!" Incidentally, the adverb form, *wryly*, is one of our personal favorite words of all time.

Witty [*adjective*]

`DEFINITION:` clever

Dr. Anna Manetta's **witty** observations on the mating dance of the naked mole rat caused more than one biologist to cackle with lusty delight.

SYNONYMS: **wry**, droll
ANTONYMS: dumb, obtuse

Reign [*verb or noun*]

as verb

DEFINITION: to hold supreme, to rule

King Lügeschnitzel **reigned** over his people with a brutal hand until the day he thankfully died from a case of uncontrollable evil laughter.

SYNONYMS: govern, dominate

as noun

DEFINITION: The time during which a leader rules

During the long, long **reign** of King Lügeschnitzel, absolutely nothing interesting happened.

SYNONYM: term of office

Notes We don't know how many times we've had to set people straight about the evil triplets *reign, rein,* and *rain.* The first one always relates to monarchs (hence the related words *regent*—a ruler, and *regicide*—the killing of a monarch). A *rein* is a leather strap used to lead a horse. And if you don't know what *rain* is, you probably shouldn't be taking the SAT next month.

Supercilious [*adjective*]

DEFINITION: uncaringly arrogant

Unlike many rich people, Gilbert Worthington III is not **supercilious** toward the suffering of the poor; in fact, he's been known to bus them in for bubble baths and pillow fights.

SYNONYMS: **haughty**, condescending
ANTONYMS: caring, humble

Haughty [adjective]

DEFINITION: overly proud

I have every right to take a **haughty**, holier-than-thou tone with you. I'm the freakin' assistant manager at Admiral Greaseburger!

SYNONYMS: arrogant, **supercilious**
ANTONYMS: modest, down-to-earth

Duped [verb]

DEFINITION: fooled or tricked

Facing almost certain death, Gretchen tried to trick the tiger by pretending she was dead. The beast was not **duped**, however, and promptly devoured her.

SYNONYMS: cheat, deceive
ANTONYM: treat honestly

Notes The noun form of the verb *dupe* is spelled the same way but has a slightly different meaning. A *dupe* is a gullible person on whom a trick is being played or who is being cheated. See "The Real Me" for more information about our friend, the noun form of *dupe*.

Deluded [verb]

DEFINITION: deceived or misled

Though often the victim of his kid sister's practical jokes, Arbuckle could not be **deluded** into swallowing a third box of woodscrews.

SYNONYMS: tricked, fooled

Notes Often we see this word applied when someone is fooling themselves, as in *self-deluded*.

The noun form *delusion* is also common, though it differs slightly in meaning from illusion. While an illusion is a mistaken belief or a hallucination, *delusion* usually has the stronger sense of being crazy or psychotic.

Also, don't confuse this word with the similar-sounding *elude*, which means "to avoid" or "escape from."

Provoke [*verb*]

DEFINITION: to stir up

Egbert playfully poked the back of Leslie's neck with his crayon, until, **provoked** to violence, Leslie turned and casually chopped his desk in two.

SYNONYMS: incite, arouse
ANTONYMS: **inhibit**, suppress

> **Notes** *Provoke* usually has the sense of baiting or irritating someone or something to action. It's often used when something controversial is being discussed, as in "*provoke* a debate." It can sometimes be used more neutrally or even positively as in "*provoke* laughter."
>
> The noun form, *provocation*, means an action that stimulates a response, usually a hostile one.
>
> Be careful not to confuse *provoke* with its very similar twin, *evoke*. When you *evoke* something, you call it into being, as in "*evoke* an image of times gone by." Often it is used with art or the imagination. It can also be used in the sense of summoning a spirit or recalling a memory.
>
> The other relative, *convoke*, more narrowly means to call a meeting or bring people together.

Persecution [*noun*]

DEFINITION: the abuse of a person or group because of their beliefs or appearance

After centuries of harassment and **persecution** for their unusual diet, the dedicated community of Swedish Leech-Eaters fled their homeland to find safety—and bounty—in the swamps of Mississippi.

SYNONYMS: oppression, discrimination
ANTONYM: equal treatment

> **Notes** Although we often see this word used in really serious cases, such as the racial or religious *persecution* of large groups of people, it can also be applied to individual cases of bullying or abuse if the victim is singled out because he or she is different in some way.

Sycophant [noun]

DEFINITION: someone who is overly flattering to authority figures

Jim is a terrible **sycophant**, constantly cleaning the soles of his boss's shoes with the inside of his lips.

SYNONYMS: toady, brown-noser

Notes   You might occasionally see the adjective form, *sycophantic*: "Jim's *sycophantic* behavior will no doubt earn him a nice corner office, a private secretary, and the disgust of all his coworkers."

Pronounce it *SICK-o-fant*, not *SEYE-ko-fant*.

Unsound [adjective]

DEFINITION 1: unstable

That wooden bridge looks rickety and **unsound**. You go first.

SYNONYM: flimsy
ANTONYMS: well-built, solid

DEFINITION 2: not valid or true

While an advertiser's assertion that "the more you spend, the more you save" might at first seem reasonable, the logic is in fact completely **unsound**.

SYNONYMS: illogical, incorrect
ANTONYMS: accurate, convincing

Notes   No, this word has nothing to do with noise. The word *sound* as an adjective means "sturdy," "reliable," or "sensible." *Unsound*, therefore, means just the opposite of all that.

Fluid [*adjective*]

DEFINITION: flowing

In one swift, **fluid** motion, the shark turned and swallowed whole the world's first scuba-monkey.

SYNONYMS: smooth, graceful
ANTONYMS: clumsy, awkward

Notes   The world's first scuba-monkey was not, in fact, eaten by a shark. Her name was Bubbles and she died of pneumonia. But we needed a decent sentence.

Plethora [*noun*]

DEFINITION: a large amount

There's a **plethora** of reasons why I won't kiss you, Mitzi, the main one being that your dental hygiene is—well—medieval.

SYNONYMS: bounty, abundance
ANTONYMS: scarcity, shortage

Notes   *Plethora* can mean simple abundance, but it can also be used to mean an overabundance or excess. You'll be pleased to know that the word's primary meaning is a medical condition in which the patient suffers from an excess of blood, giving him or her a swollen and reddish appearance. Nice, huh? Don't worry; that meaning won't appear on your test.

Irascible [*adjective*]

DEFINITION: easily irritated

Standing in line can make anyone **irascible**, which is why I always cut right to the front.

SYNONYMS: hot-tempered, testy
ANTONYMS: **tranquil**, even-tempered

Notes   A key to remembering this word is the syllable *rasc*, which is the prefix of *rascal*, a mischievous or dishonest person.

Querulous [*adjective*]

DEFINITION: whiny, complaining

Though Julius had been a **querulous**, argumentative child, years of shock therapy had turned him into an agreeable, if somewhat mush-headed, adult.

SYNONYMS: petulant, snappy
ANTONYMS: agreeable, quiescent

Notes Don't be distracted by the word's prefix, which might remind you of *query*, meaning "to question." The prefix of *querulous* is from the Latin, *queri*—"to complain."

LYRIC FREAKS!

Directions: Fill in the blanks with a word (or words) from the lyrics.

1. She was _____ , she was bold
to the point of rudeness

a. unsound
b. deluded
c. presumptuous
d. irascible
e. querulous

2. I want to be duped again

I want to be _____ again

a. used
b. fooled
c. moved
d. misused
e. bruised

3. She had a _____ way about her,
a flowing way about her, a
_____ way about her

a. fragile
b. witty
c. haughty
d. deluded
e. fluid

4. Loving her could be unnerving

She often made me _____

a. cautious
b. murderous
c. vicious
d. nervous
e. raucous

5. She could be so _____ , so
_____ , so irritable

a. deluded—mislead
b. supercilious—haughty
c. wry—unnerving
d. irascible—querulous
e. superficial—witty

PLUG IN!

Directions: Draw lines to match each word (or words) on the left to the correct definition on the right.

1 Presumptuous

2 Subtlety

3 Superficial

4 Unnerving

5 Wry

6 Witty

7 Reign

8 Supercilious

9 Duped

10 Persecution

11 Sycophant

12 Unsound

13 Fluid

14 Plethora

15 Irascible

16 Querulous

a. Flowing

b. Dry, ironic

c. Whiny, complaining, argumentative

d. Abuse due to beliefs

e. Brown-noser

f. Clever

g. Causing nervousness or fear

h. Surface-level

i. Irritable

j. Unhealthy, unstable, or illogical

k. Delicacy, artfulness, or elusiveness

l. Fooled, tricked

m. Rule with supreme power

n. Extremely bold

o. Large amount

p. Uncaring, arrogant

AMP IT UP!

Directions: Fill in the blanks, choosing the word (or words) that best completes the meaning of the sentence.

1. By criticizing the lecturer's ideas, George was trying to _____ some intelligent debate, but the speaker was so _____ by George's comments that he could barely respond.

    a. persecute—duped
    b. suggest—strengthened
    c. force—embittered
    d. provoke—unnerved
    e. escape—overwhelmed

2. Annette was an avid collector of fine art and owned a _____ of paintings and sculptures.

    a. sycophant
    b. plethora
    c. category
    d. dearth
    e. list

3. I've always found the _____, understated plumage of white doves more appealing than the _____ displays of peacocks.

    a. fragile—voluminous
    b. serene—superficial
    c. haughty—snobby
    d. sparse—plentiful
    e. subtle—showy

4. If John were less _____ and just treated us like equals, he'd probably have more friends.

    a. presumptuous
    b. haughty
    c. superficial
    d. irascible
    e. silly

5. Once again, we've _____ Alice with a bit of clever trickery.

    a. deprived
    b. insulted
    c. unnerved
    d. duped
    e. provoked

ANSWER KEY

Lyric Freaks!

1) c; 2) b; 3) e; 4) d; 5) d

Plug In!

1) n; 2) k; 3) h; 4) g; 5) b; 6) f; 7) m;
8) p; 9) l; 10) d; 11) e; 12) j; 13) a;
14) o; 15) i; 16) c

Amp It Up!

1. d

In this case, George is trying to stir up a little controversy. The best word to describe this is *provoke* (*Sometimes she'd provoke me/She'd arouse me into action*). His attempt fails, though, because the speaker whom he's trying to provoke gets so flustered, or *unnerved*, he can't even speak (*Loving her could be unnerving/She often made me nervous*). Choice a is incorrect because although George is critical, he isn't *persecuting* the speaker. Choice c is wrong because *embittered* people don't necessarily have a problem responding to whatever's bothering them.

2. b

Annette is an avid collector and will have lots of whatever she collects. Which word means "a lot"? *Plethora* (*She had a plethora of talent, a whole lot of talent...*). *Dearth* means exactly the opposite: a lack of. Choice e is a possible answer—collectors often have lists of what's in their collections, but it's not the best answer because a collector doesn't necessarily need lists in order to collect.

3. e

For the first blank, we're looking for a word that means "understated." Well, that eliminates choices a and c. Now, the sentence suggests that the answer for the second blank is the opposite of the first. In this case, choice e is correct because *showy* is the opposite of *understated*, and also the opposite of *subtle* (*But there was always so much subtlety/I never noticed how she treated me*).

4. b

In this sentence, John is acting like he's better than other people. Arrogant. Condescending. Which word is closest in meaning to *arrogant*? *Haughty* (*She could be supercilious, so haughty, she looked down on me*).

5. d

The keywords here are *clever trickery*. If someone is the victim of trickery, they are *duped* (*I want to be duped again/I want to be fooled again*). The trickery may have had an *unnerving* effect on Alice. It may have *insulted* her, *provoked* her, or even *deprived* her of something. But nothing in the sentence indicates that. Regardless of how she feels, we know she's been *duped*.

Now Playing

6

AISLE ADMISSION
CONCERT

COALESCE

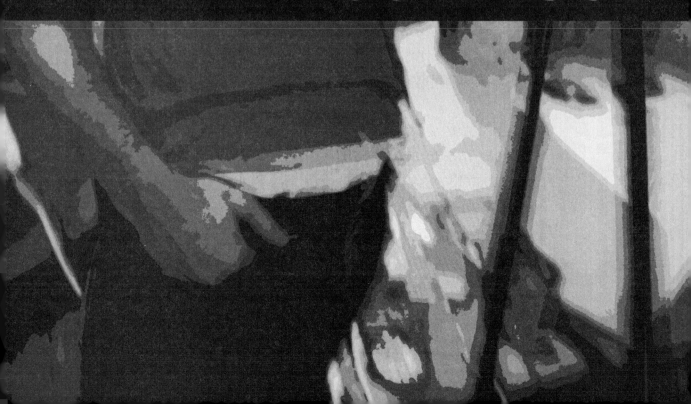

Coalesce

Let me **extol** you
Laud you and **revere** you
Venerate and worship you
Can I **cajole** you
Coax you, baby sway you
What can I do to alter you

Well I **commiserate**, I have sympathy
You know I care for you
I feel what you feel, I've got **empathy**
Girl, all you got to do

(is) **Coalesce**, unite, put it all together
Acquiesce, comply, give in to your desire
Coalesce, unite, put it all together
Acquiesce, comply, give in to your desire

Subjugate me
Domineer me, dominate me
Tell me exactly what to do
Humiliate me
Abase me and **berate** me
Treat me cruel, I'll still love you

I have **fortitude** and **longevity**
I'm strong and I'll last long for you
Don't be curt or **brusque**, don't be short with me
I'm determined, **tenacious**, **resolute**

(so) **Coalesce**, unite, put it all together
Acquiesce, comply, give in to your desire
Coalesce, unite, put it all together
Acquiesce, comply, give in to your desire

I am **ebullient**
I'm overflowing with excitement
I'm **versatile**, I do it all
My love's reliable
Well it's not fleeting or **ephemeral**
And it will be there when you fall

Cause I am everywhere, I am **ubiquitous**
You know I'm watching you
I don't miss a detail, I'm **meticulous**
Girl I'd love to study you

(so) **Coalesce**, unite, put it all together
Acquiesce, comply, give in to your desire
Coalesce, unite, put it all together
Acquiesce, comply, give in to your desire

Extol [*verb*]

`DEFINITION:` to praise highly

Verena's refusal to date you, even after I **extolled** your virtues, suggests that you should take care of that little fungal problem already.

SYNONYMS: **laud**, commend
ANTONYMS: curse, condemn

Laud [*verb*]

`DEFINITION:` to praise or compliment

Although I **laud** your noble attempts to rescue animals in distress, I really wish you'd stop trying to free my goldfish.

SYNONYMS: **extol**, applaud
ANTONYMS: criticize, **denounce**

`Notes` *Laud* is easy to remember when you realize that it's part of the word *applaud*. They're practically synonyms.

You might occasionally run across the adjective *laudatory*, which describes something that gives praise: "The *laudatory* letter you received from the Humane Society praises your effort to liberate animals, but ignores the inconvenient fact that you've killed dozens of innocent goldfish, some of whom were very high-ranking members of my aquarium."

Revere [verb]

DEFINITION: to respect highly; worship

I command you to **revere** me. On your knees, you filthy little grub!

SYNONYMS: **extol, venerate**
ANTONYMS: revile, hate

Notes This one has several common forms, like the adjectives *revered* and *reverent*. *Revered* describes the person who is respected, while *reverent* describes the person who gives respect: "The *revered* King Lügeschnitzel appeared before his *reverent* subjects to announce that he'd decided to outlaw the letter X. 'It's too eggciting,' he said."

There's the noun *reverence*, which means deep respect or adoration. It's no accident that the word is applied to clergy; a *reverend* is a leader of high status in some religious communities.

If things get sticky, just remember: "The patriots deeply respected Paul Revere for warning them that the British were coming."

Venerate [verb]

DEFINITION: to treat with admiration or awe

I, your Most High Lord and Majesty Whom You Worship and **Venerate**, demand that you bring a funny dancing monkey to delight me.

SYNONYMS: adore, **revere**
ANTONYMS: demean, insult

Notes *Veneration* is the noun form, and *venerable* is the common adjective, often used to describe wise elders: "The *venerable* old librarian, Mr. Chisworth, who had spent his life reading the great books of Western civilization, would never publicly admit that he preferred *Cosmo* to *Vogue*."

Cajole [verb]

DEFINITION: to persuade, often using insincere promises

Had Cindy not **cajoled** Roger into her house with promises of a Mexican dinner, he wouldn't now be tied to the bedpost, smeared with guacamole and awaiting what she mysteriously called "The Burrito Game."

SYNONYMS: sweet-talk, coax
ANTONYMS: dissuade, talk out of

Commiserate [verb]

DEFINITION: to express sorrow for another

Though everyone **commiserated** over Maxwell's death, we agreed he shouldn't have sampled those wild mushrooms growing near the power plant.

SYNONYMS: empathize, pity
ANTONYM: disregard

Notes   If you break this one down, it's easy to remember. You can hear the word *misery* in there. Add to it the *co-* prefix, which means "to share," and you have *co-misery*: sharing your misery with another (which is always better than sucking it up by yourself).

The noun form, *commiseration,* might slip into an SAT someday, but the verb is more common.

Empathy [noun]

DEFINITION: the ability to share in another's feelings

I have **empathy** for Maxwell; I once accidentally ate a wild mushroom that sent me into violent fits of hurling, so I sort of know what he went through.

SYNONYMS: understanding, compassion
ANTONYMS: coldness, **indifference**

Notes *Empathy* is not the same as *sympathy.* When you *sympathize* with someone, you may understand his or her feelings, but you may not share them at the moment. When you *empathize*, you feel what another person feels, usually as a result of a shared experience.

The adjective forms, *empathic* and *empathetic,* are common. (They mean the same thing. Some people just can't resist using more letters.) More rare is the word *empath*, a person with the ability to experience another person's feelings.

Coalesce [verb]

DEFINITION: to unite into a whole

We watched in horror as thousands of small globs of Play-Doh **coalesced** into a monstrous likeness of Barney the purple dinosaur, which then trampled through the fleeing mob chanting, "You Love Me."

SYNONYMS: join, combine
ANTONYMS: dissolve, disperse

Notes Implied in the word *coalesce* is the process of something coming together over time.

Acquiesce [verb]

DEFINITION: to agree to or accept

After months of pressure from parents and religious organizations, the controversial rap group Yo' Big Mama **acquiesced** to changing its name to Little Joey and the Lollipop Boys.

SYNONYMS: comply, give in
ANTONYMS: resist, oppose

Notes Implied in the word *acquiesce* is the idea that an agreement was reached unwillingly, after pressure had been applied. It has the sense of "giving in" to a request or demand.

The adjective *acquiescent* describes a person who has reluctantly agreed to something.

The related word *quiescent* describes someone or something that is agreeable and easy to control (notice the word *quiet* in there?).

Subjugate [verb]

DEFINITION: to dominate or conquer

Now that the human race had been **subjugated** after a drawn-out war, the reindeer turned against their most hated foe: Santa Claus and his horde of small but well-armed elves.

SYNONYMS: **vanquish**, defeat
ANTONYMS: surrender, lose to

Domineer [*verb*]

DEFINITION: to rule over or control

Stop trying to **domineer** me; I'm perfectly capable of chewing my own food.

SYNONYMS: bully, tyrannize
ANTONYMS: liberate, emancipate

Notes A person might be called *domineering* if they try to control others.

This one's easy to remember when you compare it against other words with the same root, like *dominate* and *dominion*.

Abase [*verb*]

DEFINITION: to embarrass

Shana said she'd go out with Jeremy only if he publicly **abased** himself by lip-synching "Like a Virgin" in the senior talent show.

SYNONYMS: humiliate, degrade
ANTONYM: earn respect

Notes Usually, a person *abases* himself or herself. It's not commonly used these days to mean "embarrass others." The noun form, *abasement*, is quite often used this way, as in *self-abasement*.

Variations of the word have similar meanings: *debase* means "to humiliate," and *base* as an adjective means "degraded," "corrupt," or "shameful"—a nice all-around word to use against anything you don't like much.

Berate [*verb*]

DEFINITION: to scold angrily

You miserable slime-sucking insect! You scummy, fat-lipped bag of ugly! You putrid, festering, worm-eaten rodent! Now kiss me, or I will continue to **berate** you!

SYNONYMS: rebuke, reprimand
ANTONYMS: praise, acclaim

Fortitude [*noun*]

DEFINITION: mental strength, moral courage

Jesper loved eating lobster, but if he'd had more **fortitude** in the face of his hunger, he would have waited until it was dead.

SYNONYMS: mettle, valor
ANTONYMS: weakness, spinelessness

Notes Another easy one to remember if you imagine the impenetrable strength of a *fortress*, which shares the root of *fortitude*.

Longevity [*noun*]

DEFINITION: long life

Congressman Kensington was admired for his **longevity**, but by age 102, his vacant stares and constant references to his Jamaican nurse, Bongi, had become a distraction on the House floor.

SYNONYMS: durability, endurance
ANTONYM: fleetingness

Brusque [*adjective*]

DEFINITION: harshly blunt

Luisa bluntly ended her marriage to Randall with a **brusque**, "I no like you face. You ugly face."

SYNONYMS: curt, short
ANTONYM: polite

Notes *Brusque* people may not be intentionally rude. They're just so direct and abrupt that they're often interpreted as harsh.

From this word we get our modern phrase "give someone the brush-off"; our word *brush* comes from *brusque*, an old French word for "broom."

Tenacious [*adjective*]

DEFINITION: stubborn and determined

Vladimir was **tenacious** in his pursuit of the world's championship in chess: He never gave up, never backed down, never lost his cool, and never won a single match.

SYNONYMS: persistent, **resolute**
ANTONYMS: undetermined, easily discouraged

Notes You might also see the word in its noun form, *tenacity*: "Vivian has the *tenacity* of a pit bull terrier; once she clamps down on a juicy piece of meat, you'd need an iron lever to pry her off."

Resolute [adjective]

DEFINITION: strong-willed or determined

I am **resolute** in my opposition to candidate Blitzer's position. Although it would be nice to connect Alaska to the motherland, it's not a good enough reason to invade Canada.

SYNONYMS: steady, firm
ANTONYMS: weak, wishy-washy

Notes You'll often see this word as the noun *resolution*: "I'm determined to stick by my New Year's *resolution*: I will not put Spam on my ice cream, no matter how much Satan wants me to."

The verb *resolve*, which means "to promise," is also common: "I hereby *resolve* to stop cheating in math class—unless I can keep getting away with it." Be careful not to confuse this with the other meaning of *resolve*, which means "to end a conflict or problem."

Ebullient [adjective]

DEFINITION: joyous and energetic

My beagle, Rex, is always **ebullient** when I come home, jumping on me, wagging his tail, and getting jiggy with my leg.

SYNONYMS: ecstatic, **jubilant**
ANTONYMS: listless, **melancholy**

Versatile [adjective]

DEFINITION: having many different skills, talents, or uses

That thing's really **versatile**! You can use it as both a toothbrush *and* a toilet scrubber. Preferably in that order.

SYNONYMS: flexible, adaptable
ANTONYMS: narrow, limited

Notes People can be *versatile* if they have different abilities and talents; things are *versatile* if they have many applications or uses. Be on the lookout for the noun form, *versatility*.

Ephemeral [*adjective*]

DEFINITION: fleeting, short-lived

This new health kick you're on is just an **ephemeral** phase; you'll be back to hoovering cheese steaks and fried dough within a week.

SYNONYMS: temporary, brief
ANTONYMS: long-lived, enduring

Ubiquitous [*adjective*]

DEFINITION: occurring everywhere, very common

The cockroach is the planet's most **ubiquitous** insect, showing up in closets, basements, and law offices the world over.

SYNONYMS: universal, omnipresent
ANTONYMS: rare, uncommon

> **Notes** The noun form is *ubiquity*, a great word to throw out at a party (if you want all other conversation to stop instantly while people stare at you): "The cockroaches' *ubiquity* in my house doesn't bother me much any more, but it still bugs me when they leave the toilet seat up."

Meticulous [*adjective*]

DEFINITION: extremely attentive to detail

Monty is **meticulous** about his hygiene. After washing with soap, he scrapes his entire body with a sterile dental pick.

SYNONYMS: exact, thorough
ANTONYMS: careless, imprecise

LYRIC FREAKS!

Directions: Fill in the blanks with a word (or words) from the lyrics.

1. I'm _____, I do it all

   a. meticulous
   b. ubiquitous
   c. ephemeral
   d. versatile
   e. brusque

2. Humiliate me
   _____ me and _____ me.
   Treat me cruel, I'll still love you

   a. Dominate—domineer
   b. Laud—commiserate
   c. Abase—berate
   d. Cajole—revere
   e. Venerate—domineer

3. I feel what you feel, I've got
   _____

   a. empathy
   b. versatility
   c. fortitude
   d. subjugation
   e. longevity

4. I am ebullient
   I'm _____

   a. filled with disappointment
   b. hiding in the basement
   c. searching for enjoyment
   d. overflowing with excitement
   e. saddened by bereavement

5. I don't _____, I'm meticulous

   a. brag about myself
   b. stop and give up
   c. believe in anything
   d. worry if I fail
   e. miss a detail

PLUG IN!

Directions: Draw lines to match each word (or words) on the left to the correct definition on the right.

1. Extol, Laud
2. Revere, Venerate
3. Cajole
4. Commiserate
5. Empathy
6. Coalesce
7. Acquiesce
8. Subjugate, Domineer
9. Abase
10. Berate
11. Fortitude
12. Longevity
13. Brusque
14. Tenacious, Resolute
15. Ebullient
16. Versatile
17. Ephemeral
18. Ubiquitous
19. Meticulous

a. Having many different skills or uses
b. Sympathize
c. Scold angrily
d. Humiliate, embarrass
e. Attentive to detail
f. Long-lasting
g. Occurring everywhere, common
h. Strength
i. Praise
j. Joyous, energetic, excited
k. Determined
l. The ability to share another's feelings
m. Fleeting, short-lived
n. Unite
o. Respect highly, worship
p. Short, curt, harshly blunt
q. Sway, persuade, coax
r. Give in, agree to
s. Dominate, rule over

AMP IT UP!

Directions: Fill in the blanks, choosing the word (or words) that best completes the meaning of the sentence.

1. Either the people will _____ to our demands, or our army will _____ them and make them serve us.

   a. hear—cajole
   b. revere—employ
   c. acquiesce—subjugate
   d. abase—domineer
   e. assume—laud

2. Richard's mother spent 15 minutes _____ him in front of everyone for coming home late. She can be so _____ sometimes.

   a. abusing—empathetic
   b. berating—domineering
   c. extolling—difficult
   d. scolding—appropriate
   e. cajoling—brusque

3. After months of gifts, sweet letters, and persistence, Ashley finally _____ David into going to the prom with her.

   a. berated
   b. cajoled
   c. acquiesced
   d. tempted
   e. abased

4. The coach's _____ personality and short temper actually served to motivate the team, as they were persistent and _____ in pursuing the State Championship.

   a. brusque—tenacious
   b. witty—smart
   c. difficult—meticulous
   d. domineering—fearful
   e. loving—resolute

5. I am absolutely _____ in my determination to become a professional musician, and nothing can stop me.

   a. meticulous
   b. ebullient
   c. versatile
   d. ephemeral
   e. resolute

ANSWER KEY

Lyric Freaks!

1) d; 2) c; 3) a; 4) d; 5) e

Plug In!

1) i; 2) o; 3) q; 4) b; 5) l; 6) n; 7) r; 8) s;
9) d; 10) c; 11) h; 12) f; 13) p 14) k;
15) j; 16) a; 17) m; 18) g; 19) e

Amp It Up!

1. c

Here's a nasty villain demanding complete subservience. If you were to put your own words in the blanks, what might they be? How about something like *agree* and *conquer*. Which answer choice best fits those words? Choice c, because *acquiesce* means "to give in" (which is much like *agree*), and *subjugate* means "to conquer" (*Subjugate me/Domineer me, dominate me*).

2. b

Immediately, you can get rid of choice c because we know Richard's mom is saying some bad stuff, not praising him, which is what *extolling* means (*Let me extol you/Laud you and revere you/Venerate and worship you*). Then we can trash choices a and d because she isn't being either *empathetic* or *appropriate*—just the opposite, in fact. That leaves us with choices b and e. The best answer is choice b because the meaning of *cajole* is closer to *persuade*, while *berate* hits the nail on the head (*Abase me and berate me/Treat me cruel, I'll still love you*).

3. b

Here, we're looking for a word that means "persuade." Why choose *cajoled* over *tempted*? You can tempt people without trying to persuade them to do something. *Cajole*, on the other hand, is synonymous with *persuade*, so it's the best answer (*Can I cajole you/Coax you, baby sway you*).

4. a

This was tough because there are so many words with similar meanings, but none as precise as choice a. We can immediately toss out choices b and e, because they have nothing to do with being short-tempered. Choice d is wrong because why would the team be *fearful*? Choice a is better than choice c because the team is *tenacious* much more than they are *meticulous*, as indicated by the keyword *persistent* (*I am determined, tenacious, resolute*).

5. e

While *meticulous* feels like it might work, being detail oriented has nothing to do with being determined. *Resolute* is close in meaning to *determined* (*I am determined, tenacious, resolute*).

7

SPITBALL IN THE EYE

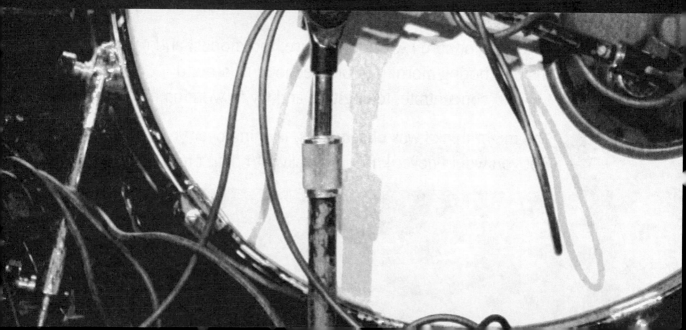

Spitball in the Eye

I knew something was **impending**, it was just about to happen
I knew some event was **imminent** when I crawled out of bed
   today
The school bus was **cacophonous** with lots of noise and
   dissonance
It was a frantic and **frenetic** mess, that's when you turned my way

If I were social and **gregarious**, I would have said, "Hello,
Who are you? Where on earth did you come from?
And where do you want to go?"

You hit me like a spitball in the eye
A spitball in the eye
That's not **facetious**, I'm not joking
I felt like I could cry
Like getting hit with a spitball in the eye

I could not hide my **chagrin**, I was embarrassed and **abashed**
   around you
I thought for sure I was too **demure**, too modest and reserved
Insipid, boring morning chatter echoed all around
I had to concentrate, to **cogitate** and try to work up my nerve

You might think I was **obsequious**, fawning over you
But you would never know I was alive if I didn't make a move

You hit me like a spitball in the eye
A spitball in the eye
That's not **facetious**, I'm not joking
I felt like I could cry
Like getting hit with a spitball in the eye

And I have been **beguiled**
Yes, I've been tricked before
And it was so **baneful**
Too deadly to ignore
If I were more **stolid**
If I didn't show emotion
If I were more **stoic**
Wouldn't feel all this commotion

You were so **tangible**, so **palpable**, you seemed to be so
    touchable
It was all chaotic, but I was so **quixotic**, I was such a romantic fool
I looked around for some **redress**, some remedy for my
    distress
But then I realized to my surprise that we were already at the
    school

If I had **summoned** all my strength, called it forth for you
Who knows where we would be right now or what our love
    could do

You hit me like a spitball in the eye
A spitball in the eye
That's not **facetious**, I'm not joking
I felt like I could cry
Like getting hit with a spitball in the eye

THE WORD ON THE WORDS

Impending [adjective]

DEFINITION: about to take place

The **impending** asteroid strike sent the people of Earth scrambling for one last taste of sweet lovin'.

SYNONYMS: **imminent**, approaching
ANTONYM: indefinite

Notes   Like the next word, *imminent*, *impending* usually suggests menace or danger, something "hanging over your head." It's no accident that the word *pend*, the root of *impend*, means "to hang," as in *pendulum* or *pendant*.

Imminent [adjective]

DEFINITION: about to take place

Anticipating fantastic wealth from the **imminent** success of *Rock the SAT*, its authors blew their life savings on plastic surgery and mad bling.

SYNONYMS: **impending**, approaching

Notes   *Imminence* suggests something that's going to happen both definitely and soon. It's often (but not always) used in the sense of a threat; a bad thing that's going to happen, as in *imminent* danger.

Be careful about the word *immanent*. Although it differs by only one letter, it means something completely different from *imminent*. *Immanent* describes the basic nature of a thing, an inherent quality. It is very unlikely (though not impossible) that you'll see it on your SAT, but you should be aware of the difference.

Cacophonous [adjective]

DEFINITION: harsh and grating to the ears

The street was a **cacophonous** jumble of horns, sirens, and car alarms, making it difficult for Rufus to engage in meaningful conversation with his rubber ducky.

SYNONYMS: noisy, dissonant
ANTONYMS: euphonius, harmonious

Notes The word *cacophony* sounds a lot like what it is: a confusing, harsh, and dissonant group of sounds. It comes from the Greek word for "evil," *kakos*, and the Greek word for "sound," *phony*.

Frenetic [adjective]

DEFINITION: hectic and disorganized

One megaphone and a truckload of cobras are all you need to turn a peaceful sing-along into a **frenetic**, terrified mob clawing over each other to save their pitiful little lives.

SYNONYMS: frenzied, frantic
ANTONYMS: **tranquil, serene**

Notes *Frenetic* derives from a word that means "crazy" or "delirious." People who were afflicted with *phrenitis*—a disease of the brain— often acted wildly. *Phrenitis* also gave us the synonyms for *frenetic*: *frantic* and *frenzied*. Today, *frenetic* is often used to indicate speed, as in *frenetic pace*.

Gregarious [*adjective*]

DEFINITION: social and outgoing

Gregarious and sociable to a fault, Geoffrey blindly led the conga line deep into enemy territory.

SYNONYMS: extroverted, convivial
ANTONYMS: reclusive, solitary

Notes Although most people like a good party every now and then, *gregarious* people are real social butterflies.

The root of *gregarious* is the Latin *grex*, meaning "flock or herd." It was first used to describe animals that hung out together, but now it's also a human characteristic. *Aggregate* (to collect) and *egregious* (to stand out) are connected by the same root.

Facetious [*adjective*]

DEFINITION: joking in an often clumsy or inappropriate manner

The mayor alienated the League of Women Voters by opening his speech with a **facetious** remark about how fabulous they'd all look in spandex.

SYNONYMS: jocose, amusing
ANTONYMS: serious, grave

Notes *Facetious* remarks are those that try to be funny but just come off sounding really stupid or inappropriate. It has nothing to do with the word *facet*, which means "a feature, aspect, or element," so don't get thrown off by anything the ETS might drop in to distract you.

Chagrin [*noun or verb*]

DEFINITION: distress caused by disappointment or embarrassment

Much to his **chagrin**, Sven had another "accident" in public and vowed never again to mix Pop Rocks and prune juice.

SYNONYMS: vexation, misfortune

Notes You might hear this word misused to mean "anger." It's really more sadness or annoyance caused by humiliation.

It can be used as a noun, as in the sentence above, or as a verb, meaning "to upset by embarrassment."

Abashed [*adjective or verb*]

DEFINITION: embarrassed

I'm not easily **abashed** by public displays of affection, but your dog better quit it.

SYNONYMS: humiliated, disconcerted
ANTONYMS: unabashed, bold

Notes The relative of this word, *bashful,* means "shy or timid."

Demure [adjective]

DEFINITION: reserved and tactful

Amelia's shy, **demure** personality didn't really fit her destiny as the Queen of the Evil Intergalactic Empire.

SYNONYMS: modest, discreet
ANTONYMS: brazen, immodest

Notes When you hear the word *demure*, think nineteenth-century Victorian men with shirt collars up to their chins or women whose idea of flirting was batting their eyelashes behind a lace fan. They used words like *delightful* and *charming*. *Demure* people always drink tea, prefer cats to dogs, and find the word *sexy* to be too risqué to use in casual conversation. Well, most people aren't quite this *demure* anymore, but you get the picture.

Be careful not to confuse the adjective *demure* with the verb *demur*, which means "to hesitate or delay."

Insipid [adjective]

DEFINITION: bland, dull

Grandma boiled the chicken for so long it became an **insipid**, fleshy paste that had all the flavor of a cardboard box.

SYNONYMS: tasteless, dull
ANTONYMS: exciting, flavorful

Notes Although *insipid* usually refers to the taste of food, it can be used more generally to describe anything dull or lacking originality: "I haven't had a more *insipid* conversation since I stood in line at the DMV behind a guy who could trace his ancestry back to the twelfth century—and did so out loud."

Don't confuse the word with *intrepid*, which means "courageous."

Cogitate [verb]

DEFINITION: to think deeply

While you float there and **cogitate** about what causes a shark feeding frenzy, I'll take this opportunity to swim for my bloody life.

SYNONYMS: ponder, contemplate

Notes *Cogitation* is just a fancy word for "thinking." It's part of Descartes' famous statement, "I think therefore I am," which in Latin is: "*Cogito ergo sum.*"

See the notes for *cognizant* in "Somnambulist" for more deliciousness.

Obsequious [adjective]

DEFINITION: overly flattering

Joshua believed that the best way to win Esmerelda's love was to be completely **obsequious**, groveling before her like the worm he was.

SYNONYMS: **sycophantic**, brown-nosing
ANTONYMS: assertive, noncompliant

Notes *Obsequious* people are those annoying suck-ups who fawn over others whether or not they really deserve it.

Beguiled [*verb or adjective*]

DEFINITION: past tense of *beguile*, to charm deceptively

With sweet whispers, Leslie **beguiled** Egbert into the elementary school's utility closet. Later, the janitor found what remained of Egbert bubbling in a mop bucket.

SYNONYMS: bewitched, enchanted

Notes *Guile* means "deceptiveness, slyness." *Beguile* can mean "to tempt someone with a false hope," as in the above sentence, or it can simply mean "to deceive." Often it carries the sense of some sort of magic being used to disguise the truth. *Beguiling* people are often attractive, but that surface appeal hides their dark motives.

As an adjective, *beguiled* describes a person who has been tricked: "Deceived by Leslie's innocent pigtails and big blue eyes, poor *beguiled* Egbert never saw the death stroke coming."

Baneful [*adjective*]

DEFINITION: harmful or poisonous

The venom of this black mamba snake is the most **baneful** in nature; one bite can kill a healthy man by the time he can finish this...

SYNONYMS: toxic, lethal
ANTONYMS: healing, therapeutic

Notes The noun form, *bane*, derives from an Old English word meaning "murderer." So, anything *baneful* is seriously harmful, probably fatal. Better you shouldn't play with it, dahling.

Stolid [*adjective*]

DEFINITION: expressing little emotion

While some feel that Jamison's **stolid** personality is the result of his rigid British upbringing, others blame it on the coma.

SYNONYMS: **stoic, indifferent**
ANTONYMS: emotional, expressive

Notes   Though you'll probably be reminded of *solid*, this word has more in common with *stoic*, which means "unemotional" (see below).

Stoic [*adjective or noun*]

DEFINITION: unemotional

Jorge Luis Pizarro appeared **stoic** and steely-eyed before the firing squad, but when asked if he had any last requests, he collapsed in a whimpering heap, sobbing, "Please let me go. I'll be your best friend."

SYNONYMS: **stolid**, unmoved
ANTONYMS: easily moved, emotional

Notes   Think Mr. Spock from *Star Trek*, if you're as geeky as we are. If not, this might help: we get this adjective from a group of ancient Greek philosophers, the *Stoics*, who believed that being completely unemotional was the path to deeper wisdom. Their founder, Zeno, conducted his teachings in ancient Athens on a porch, which in Greek was called a *stoa*. Hence, *Stoics*. Today, *stoicism* is more a personality trait than a philosophical study.

Tangible [*adjective*]

DEFINITION: capable of being felt

Because the police were unable to locate any **tangible** evidence of foul play—such as a murder weapon or rubber gloves—Sir Regis Watercracker was able to keep his tee time.

SYNONYMS: **palpable**, touchable
ANTONYMS: intangible, impalpable

Notes   Finally, a gift for all you math nerds. *Tangible* is related to the *tangent* in geometry, a line that "touches" a circle. So, when you see *tangible*, think "capable of being touched."

We use *tangible* to mean things we can physically feel, like a rock or a fist plowing into our foreheads, but it can also mean things that are not physical but have some substance or meat: "The science experiments, for so long merely theoretical, are finally yielding *tangible* results. Soon we shall have a race of mutant frog men to rule us with a slimy fist."

The word has absolutely nothing to do with *tangerine*, which is a fruit that originally came from Tangiers, in Morocco.

Palpable [*adjective*]

DEFINITION: capable of being felt

The tension at the treaty negotiation was **palpable** as everyone waited to see who would make a move on the last glazed donut.

SYNONYMS: **tangible**, touchable
ANTONYMS: impalpable, insubstantial

Notes   Like *tangible*, things that can be felt physically are *palpable*. But often we use the word to describe the perception of subtle energy, like tension in the above sentence. Tension isn't physical, but we can feel it; it's *palpable*. In this sense, it's closer in meaning to "easily perceived" or "evident."

Quixotic [adjective]

DEFINITION: foolishly impractical

Antoine's **quixotic** dream of being Superman led him to squeeze into his sister's leotards; admiring the fit, he decided he'd rather imitate Wonder Woman.

SYNONYMS: wild, rash
ANTONYMS: rational, practical

Notes This word comes from the comic Spanish novel *Don Quixote*. The main character, Quixote, lived in a dream world where he believed himself to be a great hero and was always embarking on impossible quests; at one point he attacked a windmill, thinking it was a dragon. The word has therefore come to describe someone who's foolishly and romantically impractical, often in an amusing way. It can also mean "unpredictable" or "impulsive."

Redress [noun or verb]

DEFINITION 1: relief from pain or distress

The only **redress** for a broken heart is to constantly pester the jerk who dumped you with obscene phone calls every hour on the hour.

SYNONYMS: remedy, reparation
ANTONYMS: injury, wrong

DEFINITION 2: compensation

Outraged vegetarians demanded **redress** from Nature's Goodsome Foods, Inc. when it was discovered that their "Hawaiian Sunrise Fruit Salad" was really just a can of guava-flavored pig eyes.

SYNONYMS: payback, restitution

Notes Whenever you *redress* a problem or insult, you're trying to set things right. There are several ways to do it: by healing the wound, paying the injured party back, or, if all else fails, taking sweet revenge.

Summoned [*verb*]

DEFINITION: past tense of *summon*, to call forth

Whenever Chinaski was **summoned** from the bench, he appeared quickly at the coach's side; although he never actually touched the ball, Chinaski's promptness was the stuff of legends.

SYNONYMS: invoked

Notes When someone *summons* you, they're usually calling you to show up for some specific purpose. Often the *summoner* holds a position of authority. In legalese, a *summons* is an order to appear in court.

LYRIC FREAKS!

Directions: Fill in the blanks with a word (or words) from the lyrics.

1. You hit me like a spitball in the eye
   A spitball in the eye
   That's not _____, I'm not joking
   I felt like I could cry

   a. facetious
   b. gregarious
   c. stoic
   d. quixotic
   e. stolid

2. If I were social and _____,
   I would have said "Hello,
   Who are you? Where on earth did you
   come from?
   And where do you want to go?"

   a. insipid
   b. cacophonous
   c. obsequious
   d. facetious
   e. gregarious

3. You might think I was obsequious,
   _____.
   But you would never know I was alive if I
   didn't make a move

   a. fawning over you
   b. pretending I'm not blue
   c. trying to start anew
   d. weeping because of you
   e. not knowing what is true

4. And I have been _____
   Yes, I've been tricked before

   a. summoned
   b. quixotic
   c. beguiled
   d. baneful
   e. stolid

5. You were so _____, so
   _____, you seemed to be
   touchable

   a. imminent–impending
   b. stolid–stoic
   c. cacophonous–frenetic
   d. tangible–palpable
   e. obsequious–facetious

PLUG IN!

Directions: Draw lines to match each word (or words) on the left to the correct definition on the right.

1	Impending, Imminent	a. Social and outgoing
2	Cacophonous	b. Embarrassed
3	Frenetic	c. Remedy, relief
4	Gregarious	d. Showing little or no emotion
5	Facetious	e. Concentrate, think deeply
6	Chagrin	f. Joking
7	Abashed	g. Deadly, harmful or poisonous
8	Demure	h. Touchable, capable of being felt
9	Insipid	i. Fawning, overly flattering
0	Cogitate	j. Boring, bland, dull
1	Obsequious	k. Overly romantic, foolishly impractical
2	Beguiled	l. Called forth
3	Baneful	m. Tricked, charmed, bewitched
4	Stolid, Stoic	n. About to happen
5	Tangible, Palpable	o. Distress caused by embarrassment or disappointment
6	Quixotic	p. Frantic, hectic, disorganized
7	Redress	q. Reserved and tactful, quiet
8	Summoned	r. Noisy, dissonant

AMP IT UP!

Directions: Fill in the blanks, choosing the word (or words) that best completes the sentence.

1. The ant is one of the more _____ insects, living in large, complex societies rather than individually.

a. demure
b. gregarious
c. stoic
d. quixotic
e. unabashed

2. After the awards ceremony, even the most well-known actors fawned over the hot, new film director hoping their _____ behavior would _____ her into casting them in her next movie.

a. facetious–trick
b. baneful–persuade
c. insipid–force
d. obsequious–beguile
e. available–cogitate

3. Charging into battle like that was perhaps the most heroic thing I've ever witnessed, but it may also have been the most foolish and _____.

a. frenetic
b. stolid
c. facetious
d. quixotic
e. noble

4. I feel very sorry for all the trouble I've put you through. Is there anything I can do to _____ your suffering?

a. summon
b. destroy
c. redress
d. abash
e. obliterate

5. Now that the approaching storm was _____, people hurried to the supermarket to stock up on supplies.

a. ferocious
b. cacophonous
c. impending
d. baneful
e. violent

ANSWER KEY

Lyric Freaks!

1) a; 2) e; 3) a; 4) c; 5) d

Plug In!

1) n; 2) r; 3) p; 4) a; 5) f; 6) o; 7) b;
8) q; 9) j; 10) e; 11) i; 12) m; 13) g;
14) d; 15) h; 16) k; 17) c; 18) l

Amp It Up!

1. b

Because the sentence states that ants live in a society, we're looking for a word that means "social." There's only one, so shout it at the top of your lungs. *Gregarious* (*If I were social and gregarious, I would have said, "Hello"*)!

2. d

Here, we're looking for a word similar to *fawn* for the first blank and *charm* for the second blank. The best choice is d, *obsequious* (*You might think I was obsequious, fawning over you*) and *beguile* (*And I have been beguiled/Yes, I've been tricked before*). Although there are synonyms for *fawn* and *charm* scattered in the other answer choices, you don't get two of them together in any other choice.

3. d

Charging into battle may have been *noble*, maybe even *frenetic*, but the keyword here is *foolish*, which is pretty close to *quixotic* (*It was all chaotic, but I was so quixotic, I was such a romantic fool*).

4. c

To *redress* is to help remedy a past wrong (*I looked around for some redress, some remedy for my distress*), which is exactly what our speaker is trying to do. The only other possibilities are choices b and e, but *destroy* and *obliterate* both mean "to erase completely," and can anyone completely erase someone's suffering? No, they can only try to make it a little better. Remember to be suspicious of the absolute words.

5. c

This one's tough because a bad storm can be described by any of these answer choices. The key here is that the storm hasn't yet hit. Maybe it will be *violent, ferocious, baneful,* or *cacophonous,* but we don't know for sure. We do know that the storm is approaching. That makes it *impending* (*I knew something was impending, it was just about to happen*).

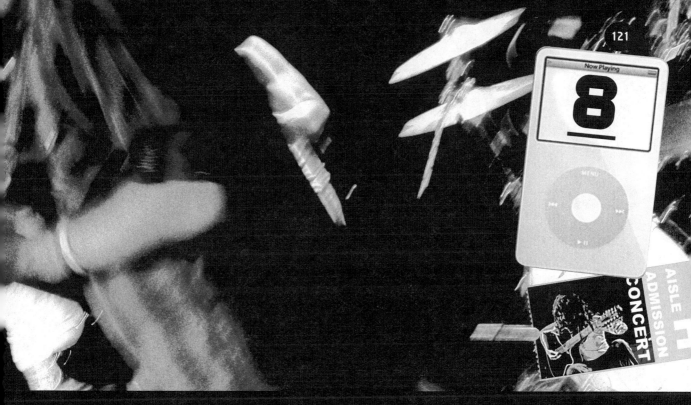

Now Playing

8

AISLE
ADMISSION
CONCERT

SALACIOUS

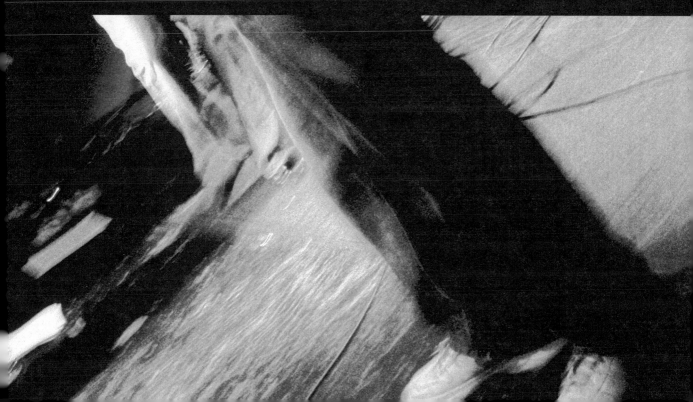

Salacious

Lately I feel **salacious**
Lecherous, **lascivious**
I'm telling you I feel lustful
And that makes me **loquacious**
Verbose and **garrulous**
I talk too much, I speak a mouthful

Is it **kismet**
Is it fate
Or are we not meant to be
Back and forth I **oscillate**
Back and forth I **vacillate**

And I don't want to confuse you
And I know I've been **mercurial**
I'm constantly changing my direction
And I don't want to lose you
But I'm **dubious**, I'm doubtful, when I'm through
Will I turn to you

Lately I feel **obstreperous**
Tumultuous, so **boisterous**
I'm telling you, I'm feeling rowdy
And that makes things **precarious**
Perilous, so dangerous
We're riding on shaky ground now

Should I **succumb** to what's tempting me
Should I give in to curiosity
Where is my **integrity**
Where is my honesty

And I don't want to confuse you
And I know I've been **capricious**
I'm constantly following my impulse
And I don't want to lose you
But I'm **dubious**, I'm doubtful, when I'm through
Will I turn to you

Or will I walk away
Will I **renounce** your love
Will I give it all away
And all this **speculation**
This guessing must be driving you crazy

Lately I feel **salacious**
Lecherous, **lascivious**
I'm telling you I'm feeling lustful
That makes things **precarious**
Perilous, so dangerous
We're riding on shaky ground now, shaky ground now

And I don't want to confuse you
And I know I've been **mercurial**
I'm constantly changing my direction
And I don't want to lose you
But I'm **dubious**, I'm doubtful, when I'm through
Will I turn to you...

Salacious [adjective]

DEFINITION: arousing lustful or obscene feelings

Kelly's rapt attention in social studies class was due more to her **salacious** fantasies about Ivan the Terrible than to any real interest in Russian history.

SYNONYMS: **lecherous, lascivious**
ANTONYM: prudish

Notes *Salacious* is frequently used to describe media such as TV programs or newspaper articles that use sexual content to attract an audience. "The *salacious* photos of the Queen of England in her bikini on page 6 of *The Enquirer* are a disgusting, shameful, and very effective way to sell papers."

Lecherous [adjective]

DEFINITION: overindulging in sexual activity

When a 70-year-old man dates a 25-year-old model, women call him a **lecherous** pervert; men call him one stoked old dude.

SYNONYMS: **lascivious**, lewd
ANTONYM: chaste

Notes The noun is *letch*. It almost always means a man, usually old, who has an unhealthy sexual interest in someone who either doesn't share it or who is not an appropriate object.

Lascivious [adjective]

DEFINITION: expressing lewdness in a distasteful way

Amber drooled with **lascivious** desire when Justin strutted through the room wearing his hall monitor sash.

SYNONYMS: wanton, **lecherous**
ANTONYM: nonsexual

Notes We just hope you all appreciate how difficult it was for us to hold back when writing sentences for *salacious*, *lecherous*, and *lascivious*. We're very proud to have produced quality G-rated material. Well, at least PG-13.

Loquacious [adjective]

DEFINITION: very talkative or wordy

Garvey was so painfully **loquacious** at the party that by the time he'd finished his fifth story, everyone had drifted off to play Twister.

SYNONYMS: **garrulous**, **verbose**
ANTONYMS: quiet, **taciturn**

Notes The noun form is either *loquacity* or the one preferred by *loquacious* people: *loquaciousness*.

What does *loquacious* have in common with *eloquent* (well-spoken), *colloquial* (using common speech), and *circumlocution* (using an excessive number of words)? They share the root, *loqui*, Latin for "to speak."

Garrulous [adjective]

DEFINITION: pointlessly or annoyingly talkative

The normally **garrulous** Larry fell silent when his date declared that if he didn't shut up, she had a roll of duct tape with his name on it.

SYNONYMS: **verbose**, **loquacious**
ANTONYMS: terse, quiet

Notes Once again, you have a choice of nouns: *garrulity* or *garrulousness*. Guess which one wins you Brownie points?

Verbose [*adjective*]

DEFINITION: excessively wordy

The fact that there are so many synonyms for **verbose** suggests that we all talk too much and should just shut up already.

SYNONYMS: **loquacious, garrulous**
ANTONYMS: terse, **laconic**

Notes Don't get confused by this word's similarity to *verb*. Think instead of *verbal*—expressing through language. If you're *verbose* you're over-the-top *verbal*.

Verbosity or *verboseness* are your nouns.

While the above three words are practically synonymous, they have subtle differences:

Loquacious describes someone who just talks a lot, but it doesn't evaluate the content of what they say.

Garrulous describes someone who not only talks often, but rambles pointlessly.

Verbose describes people who may or may not talk often, but when they do talk they use an excessive number of words.

Kismet [*noun*]

DEFINITION: fate

It must be **kismet** that a fat, juicy 'possum darted in front of my car at the very moment I had a hankering for some roadkill.

SYNONYMS: destiny, fortune

Notes This is one of the few English words on loan to us from Turkish (via Arabic). It's often used in conversation to indicate good fortune, but the word is really neutral.

Oscillate [verb]

DEFINITION: to swing back and forth

The belly-dancer **oscillated** her hips with long, hypnotic swings, distracting Sultan Rahman Al-Hakim while his harem quietly escaped into the desert night.

SYNONYMS: vary, fluctuate
ANTONYM: hold steady

Notes *Oscillations* can be either very slow, like the swinging of a giant pendulum, or rapid, like the readout on your heart rate monitor when the doctor hands you the bill for your triple bypass surgery.

Oscillations can be physical, in the sense of a thing moving back and forth between points, but they can also be abstract, such as when you go back and forth between two decisions: "Elvira *oscillated* between going out with Jerome, who was rich but ugly, and Damien, who was cute but smelled like cheese."

Vacillate [verb]

DEFINITION: to waver or be indecisive

Although I **vacillate** on many subjects, there's one thing I'm certain of: monkeys are cool.

SYNONYMS: **oscillate**, fluctuate
ANTONYMS: decide, remain firm

Notes *Vacillate* and *oscillate* are close in meaning, but *vacillate* primarily means "to be wishy-washy and uncertain," whereas *oscillate* means "to go back and forth between two options." *Oscillate* can often describe a physical object in motion, but a *vacillation* usually happens in the mind.

Mercurial [*adjective*]

DEFINITION: changing often

Glenda's **mercurial** nature is confusing. First she wants to be the wicked witch, then she wants to be the good witch, then she gets bored and wants to be the sort-of-wicked-but-not-as-wicked-as-the-wicked-witch witch.

SYNONYMS: fickle, unpredictable
ANTONYMS: unchanging, consistent

Notes Just think of *mercury*, the liquid metal. Any self-respecting metal holds its shape at room temperature, but not mercury. It's constantly changing.

Dubious [*adjective*]

DEFINITION: doubtful or questionable

Given that your apartment is strewn with fur balls and cat skulls, I find your offer to take care of Muffy while I'm gone somewhat **dubious**.

SYNONYMS: skeptical, uncertain
ANTONYMS: certain, trustworthy

Notes There are a couple of ways to use *dubious*: one is to mean "suspicious," as in the example above. Another is to mean "uncertain," as in: "I'm *dubious* as to whether we could actually defeat the Canadians even if we got the green light to invade. They have an awful lot of angry moose up there, don'tcha know."

If a person is *dubious*, it means that either he's skeptical or one should be skeptical of him. If a thing is *dubious*, then we're skeptical about it.

You've got a choice of two nouns again: *dubiousness* or *dubiety*.

Obstreperous [*adjective*]

DEFINITION: unruly and noisy

It was a crazy, crazy scene—noise, glass breaking, people hanging from chandeliers; who knew that nuns could be so **obstreperous**!

SYNONYMS: clamorous, **boisterous**
ANTONYMS: **tranquil**, **serene**

Notes It's not a common word, but it is pretty cool. We like it because it SOUNDS *obstreperous*!

Tumultuous [*adjective*]

DEFINITION: loud and violently chaotic

When it was announced that tater-tots would no longer be sold in the cafeteria, the third-graders erupted into a **tumultuous** riot that shook the very foundations of lunchroom policy.

SYNONYMS: unruly, riotous
ANTONYMS: **tranquil**, peaceful

Notes The noun form is *tumult*: "The lunch monitors were thankfully able to calm the *tumult* before it spilled out onto the street and engulfed the entire west side of town."

Boisterous [*adjective*]

DEFINITION: uncontrollably loud and rowdy

I usually don't mind cousin Becky's **boisterous** outbursts, but I cringe every Thanksgiving when she leaps on the dinner table shouting, "Stuff that turkey, baby, yeah!"

SYNONYMS: exuberant, rambunctious
ANTONYMS: sedate, mellow

Notes *Obstreperous, tumultuous,* and *boisterous* are pretty close synonyms, and if you remember that they all relate to noise, violence, or rowdiness you'll be all right. For you nitpickers out there (you know who you are), here are the differences:

Obstreperous mainly means "noisily unruly." If you're unruly but quiet, you're not *obstreperous.* It also has the sense that the unruliness isn't terribly violent or harmful. Just nutty.

Tumultuous implies something seriously chaotic, even dangerous or violent, like a war, riot, or earthquake.

Boisterous has the sense of rowdy celebration, like a party that's gotten a little out of hand. But it's not dangerous or even necessarily unpleasant (unless you weren't invited and you're trying to get some sleep in the next apartment).

Precarious [*adjective*]

DEFINITION: dangerous or unstable

After mating, the male black widow spider is in a most **precarious** position: quite possibly, the female will eat him alive. But hey, at least he dies happy.

SYNONYMS: risky, **perilous**
ANTONYMS: safe, secure

Notes *Precarious* can be used to describe physical danger, as in the sentence above. Someone in a *precarious* situation at work, though, is probably about to get canned.

Perilous [adjective]

DEFINITION: extremely dangerous

It can be quite **perilous** trying to take candy from a well-armed baby.

SYNONYMS: risky, dangerous
ANTONYM: safe

Notes *Peril* is usually serious danger: something that puts you at risk of extreme injury or even death. It's sometimes used for dramatic effect, as a kind of humorous understatement: "A deluxe double mayo-dipped deep-fried Greaseburger may be delicious, but you eat it at your own *peril*."

Succumb [verb]

DEFINITION: to give in

After a vicious fistfight, Rocco finally **succumbed** to Vittorio's overwhelming power and let him play the role of Juliet in the balcony scene.

SYNONYMS: yield, submit
ANTONYMS: resist, defy

Notes *Succumb* can be used to mean "give in to a stronger force," as in the above sentence, but it can also mean "to be brought to an end," often by some kind of outside force: "Before he *succumbed* to the effects of the poison, Socrates gurgled out his enduring final words: 'I drank whaaaa...?'"

The word's not always used negatively; you can also *succumb* to an overwhelming desire for something, like ice cream or your best friend's date.

Integrity [noun]

DEFINITION 1: moral strength or discipline

I have enough **integrity** to stand up for what I believe, as long as it's OK with my mom.

SYNONYMS: honesty, incorruptibility
ANTONYMS: dishonesty, dishonorability

DEFINITION 2: dependability

Let's hope our new ship maintains its **integrity**. I don't want a repeat of last year, what with all the sinking and dying.

SYNONYMS: soundness, stability
ANTONYMS: instability, unreliability

DEFINITION 3: wholeness

It requires the cooperation of each student to guarantee the **integrity** of the entire class. If even one of you little buggers gets out of line, I'm shipping you off to a Burmese prison camp!

SYNONYMS: completeness, togetherness
ANTONYM: incompleteness

Notes The third definition of *integrity* is somewhat related to the word *integral*, which describes a necessary part of something: "The liver is *integral* to healthy digestion; without one, things get very messy." You might also hear echoes of *integrate*, which means "to put things together into a whole."

Capricious [*adjective*]

DEFINITION: making quick, unpredictable decisions

On yet another **capricious** impulse, Esther left the nursing home to join a militant, right-wing knitting circle.

SYNONYMS: whimsical, impulsive
ANTONYMS: planned, deliberate

Notes People can be *capricious,* as in Esther's case, but decisions themselves can also be described as *capricious.*

The noun form, *caprice,* is an irrational or unpredictable desire.

The word comes from Italian; *capo-* is "head," and *–riccio* means, um, "hedgehog." We guess hedgehogs are impulsive animals. Who knew?

Renounce [*verb*]

DEFINITION: to refuse formally; to abandon

I hereby **renounce** a life spent sitting on my fat butt and dedicate myself to a strict new diet. Oh, who am I kidding? Pass the Spam loaf.

SYNONYMS: **repudiate**, reject
ANTONYM: accept

Notes The noun form is *renunciation.* It can mean "to refuse by a formal declaration," as in the above sentence, or it can mean "to refuse to recognize or obey an authority": "Vicky's *renunciation* of the school's bylaws meant that she was now free—FREE!—to answer all her teachers' questions through interpretive dance."

Speculation [*noun*]

DEFINITION: casual thought or consideration

Judging by the glazed, distant look in Sergei's eyes, he's either forming **speculations** about his future or he's really, really stupid.

SYNONYMS: pondering, contemplation

Notes *Speculation* actually has two primary meanings. The first you see in the above sentence. The other one means "to earn money by buying and selling with the hope of future profits." So, if you buy a house that you hope will appreciate in value so that you can sell it again, you're *speculating*. This meaning is less likely to appear on your SAT.

LYRIC FREAKS!

Directions: Fill in the blanks with a word (or words) from the lyrics.

1. Lately I feel _____

_____, _____

I'm telling you I feel lustful

a. obstreperous—Tumultuous—boisterous
b. loquacious—Verbose—garrulous
c. precarious—Perilous—dangerous
d. salacious—Lecherous—lascivious
e. dubious—Mercurial—capricious

2. And I know I've been _____

I'm constantly changing my direction

a. garrulous
b. mercurial
c. capricious
d. precarious
e. loquacious

3. And I know I've been _____

I'm constantly following my impulse

a. loquacious
b. capricious
c. mercurial
d. perilous
e. dubious

4. Will I renounce your love

Will I _____

a. watch it slip away
b. give it all away
c. fight another day
d. let love save the day
e. see it fade to gray

5. Should I _____ to what's tempting me

Should I give in to curiosity

a. succumb
b. kismet
c. oscillate
d. vacillate
e. renounce

PLUG IN!

Directions: Draw lines to match each word (or words) on the left to the correct definition on the right.

1. Salacious, Lecherous, Lascivious   a. Guesswork, casual thought

2. Loquacious, Garrulous, Verbose   b. To waver or be indecisive

3. Kismet   c. Doubtful

4. Oscillate   d. Dangerous

5. Vacillate   e. Fate

6. Mercurial   f. To give away or reject

7. Dubious   g. Talkative

8. Obstreperous, Tumultuous, Boisterous   h. Honesty, moral strength

9. Precarious, Perilous   i. Constantly changing

10. Succumb   j. Rowdy

11. Integrity   k. Making quick decisions based on impulse

12. Capricious   l. Give in

13. Renounce   m. To swing back and forth

14. Speculation   n. Lustful

AMP IT UP!

Fill in the blanks, using the word (or words) that best completes the meaning of the sentence.

1. Douglas was considered a _____ person for always changing his mind, because he would always _____ between different alternatives.

a. salacious—choose
b. garrulous--argue
c. mercurial—vacillate
d. speculative—guess
e. capricious—remain

2. After Brother Albert _____ his attachment to the monastery, he became a famous university professor in France.

a. renounced
b. succumbed
c. disbanded
d. reinforced
e. speculated

3. I'm _____ about your desire to go to medical school; are you doing it for yourself or for your parents?

a. loquacious
b. capricious
c. obstreperous
d. perilous
e. dubious

4. If you follow your impulses and live a life of _____, you may eventually find yourself without a stable future, living _____ from paycheck to paycheck.

a. wandering—dubiously
b. lechery—tumultuously
c. speculation—delicately
d. caprice—precariously
e. responsibility—mercurially

5. At mating time, the male ducks chase the female ducks _____.

a. precariously
b. lasciviously
c. relentlessly
d. boisterously
e. perilously

ANSWER KEY

Lyric Freaks!

1) d; 2) b; 3) b; 4) b; 5) a

Plug In!

1) n; 2) g; 3) e; 4) m; 5) b; 6) i; 7) c;
8) j; 9) d; 10) l; 11) h; 12) k; 13) f; 14)a

Amp It Up!

1. c

We know the first blank has to describe someone who changes his mind often. That leaves us with choices c and e as possibilities. The second blank must mean "moving back and forth between choices," which is the definition of *vacillate* (*Back and forth* I *vacillate*).

2. a

To *renounce* is to reject or give up, and that's what Brother Albert did when he left the monastery (*Will I renounce your love/Will I give it all away*). Choice c is the only other word that comes close, but one doesn't *disband* an attachment—one can disband a group of something, but not a single thing.

3. e

The speaker in this sentence is questioning a person's motivation for going to medical school. *Dubious*, which means "doubtful," is the best answer (*But I'm dubious, I'm doubtful, when I'm through*).

4. d

What is it to follow your impulses? *Caprice*, which is the noun form of *capricious* (*And I know I've been capricious/I'm constantly following my impulse*). What is it to live without stability? *Precariousness*. Choice a seems good at first, but how does one live *dubiously*?

5. b

We're looking for a word that suggests a sexual frenzy, because it's mating time. Since the only word with sexual connotation is *lasciviously*, it's correct, even if it is a little bit tacky (*Lately I've been salacious/Lecherous, lascivious/I'm telling you I feel lustful*).

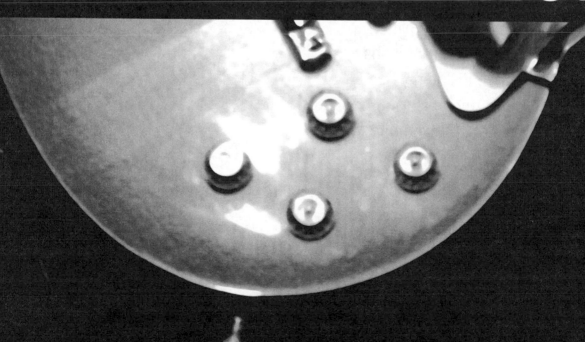

IMAGINATION

Imagination

Love is so **elusive**
Cleverly avoiding me
I search for a **blueprint**
A detailed plan to make you see
Don't you know I'm **yearning**
Longing for your eyes on me
Hear my **lamentation**
It's the expression of my grief

Love has been so **injurious** to me, it's caused me harm and
    tension
But I've a **premonition**, a feeling something soon may happen

Use your imagination
High and **lofty** visions
Dance inside my head
Heed my praise and **adulation**
Don't you **terminate** this
Don't make this the end

Love's my **panacea**
The cure-all for all my needs
Lately I've been poisoned
And you're my **antidote** it seems
Don't **exploit** my weakness
Don't you take advantage of me

Try not to insult or **deride** me
Respect my vulnerability

Love is only known by a chosen few, it seems so **esoteric**
It makes me **melancholy** and blue, if that's love then how **ironic**

Use your imagination
High and **lofty** visions
Dance inside my head
There's no time for **inhibition**
Don't hold back your emotions
Let your love shine through

I may not speak your language
Don't know your **jargon**
I might be so **gullible**, I'll believe in anything and everything
I'll **verify** my love for you
I'll prove it true
I'll prove it true

Use your imagination
High and **lofty** visions
Dance inside my head
Act upon your own **volition**
Choose what you want to do
It's what I want too

I want to be with you
Let your love shine through
Let it **emerge** from you...

Elusive [adjective]

`DEFINITION 1:` difficult to capture

While the biologists were overjoyed that the **elusive** Razor-Toothed Tiger had come into view for the first time, they greatly underestimated its lust for human flesh.

SYNONYMS: evasive, slippery
ANTONYMS: obvious, easily caught

`DEFINITION 2:` difficult to understand

I find theories of quantum hyperdimensional metaphysics somewhat **elusive**, but hot-oil wrestling? That I get.

SYNONYMS: **abstruse, esoteric**
ANTONYMS: simple, comprehensible

`DEFINITION 3:` difficult to isolate or identify

What is that **elusive** scent in your perfume...it's not...wait...it's...it's hippo musk, isn't it?

SYNONYMS: indistinguishable, indistinct
ANTONYMS: distinguishable, discrete

Notes *Elusive* is the adjective form of *elude*, which means "to escape": "The Razor-Toothed Tiger had *eluded* the scientists for months, but it finally decided to stop a-runnin' and start a-slashin'."

It often carries the sense of something mysterious or haunting.

Blueprint [noun]

DEFINITION: a plan of action or a design

My **blueprint** for world peace...let's see: protecting the environment, providing free health care and education to all, and blasting to smithereens anyone who dares oppose me.

SYNONYMS: plan, **agenda**

Notes The primary meaning of *blueprint* is the plan an architect draws up before constructing a building (so called because they're printed on blue paper). The term is often used more generally, however, to mean any kind of plan or design.

Yearning [verb or noun]

as verb

DEFINITION: desiring in a tender or sad way

Having spent years away from my home in the Himalayas, I've been **yearning** for the tart flavor of yak's milk, but alas, there are precious few yaks in downtown Detroit.

SYNONYMS: longing, craving
ANTONYM: aversion

as noun

DEFINITION: a strong desire

At last! I can satisfy my **yearning** for the cuisine of my homeland at Michigan's first and only Nepalese restaurant, *Yak Barn*.

SYNONYMS: yen, hunger

Lamentation [*noun*]

DEFINITION: a strong expression of sorrow

After Lawrence's death, his family mourned and sang **lamentations** until dawn, when they buried him out back with the other gerbils.

SYNONYMS: mourning, grieving
ANTONYM: celebration

Notes *Lamentation* is a variation of the noun *lament*, which means "to regret deeply." *Lament* doubles as the verb, which can also mean "to wail" or "cry out in sorrow." The adjective *lamentable* describes something to feel regretful over.

Injurious [*adjective*]

DEFINITION: harmful

Nelson's fascination with mucus proved **injurious** when he couldn't shake the nickname "Yuck Boy."

SYNONYMS: damaging, **deleterious**
ANTONYMS: curative, helpful

Notes This one's easy: *injurious* is the adjective form of *injury*. Got that?

Premonition [*noun*]

DEFINITION: a sense of things to come

Yesterday, I foresaw that I would get hit by a bus. Today, I'm happy to report that my **premonition** was wrong; it's actually *you* who gets nailed.

SYNONYMS: forewarning, omen

Notes *Premonitions* are different from *predictions*: *predictions* are often based on evidence or fact. A *premonition* is an intuition, a kind of extrasensory perception.

Lofty [adjective]

DEFINITION 1: high or difficult to reach

The loss of most of his skin to frostbite seemed a small price to pay for Gerald, who became the first nudist to scale the **lofty** peak of Mount Everest.

SYNONYMS: eminent, towering
ANTONYM: low

DEFINITION 2: noble and dignified

The **lofty** knight looked down at the opponent he had just skewered, and with a noble wave of his hand had the body dragged through the streets of London.

SYNONYMS: exalted, commanding
ANTONYMS: lowborn, common

Notes You can remember *lofty* from the word *loft*. As a verb, *loft* means "to throw something high in the air" or "to lob." As a noun, it is a room at the top of a house or apartment. The adjective, *aloft*, means "airborne." It's all just high, high up there.

Heed [verb or noun]

DEFINITION: to pay attention to

Stop...I said stop squirming! This is all your fault anyway—if only you'd **heeded** the warning on your medication, we wouldn't *need* to shave your tongue.

SYNONYMS: consider, regard
ANTONYMS: ignore, disregard

Notes *Heed* will very rarely appear as a noun, meaning "attention." You can use it in the same way, as in *pay heed*, or the opposite, *pay no heed*.

Adulation [*noun*]

DEFINITION: high praise, admiration

The monks deeply admired their high priest and expressed their **adulation** by throwing wild parties in his honor—and, of course, in his absence.

SYNONYMS: worship, **reverence**
ANTONYMS: disrespect, scorn

Notes *Adulation* has the sense of excessive or over-the-top flattery, kind of like the bleary-eyed, mindless worship the British display toward the royal family, no matter how weird they get.

The verb *adulate* and the adjective *adulatory* are less common, but you better know 'em.

Terminate [*verb*]

DEFINITION: to end

Famed psychologist Dr. Simon Bouvier **terminated** his experiments when his new antidepressant drug turned his test subjects into homicidal (though happy) maniacs.

SYNONYMS: complete, conclude
ANTONYMS: continue, prolong

Panacea [*noun*]

DEFINITION: a cure-all

Candidate Blitzer's solution is not a **panacea** for every problem in America, though it would be cool to conquer the Canadians.

SYNONYM: remedy

Notes Most of the time, the word *panacea* is used to indicate some kind of magical or mythical ideal cure that cannot in reality exist.

Antidote [noun]

DEFINITION: something that relieves or reverses

Billionaire Gilbert Worthington III was hard-pressed to find **antidotes** for the 47 different poisons his servants had slipped into his milk and cookies.

SYNONYMS: palliative, antitoxin
ANTONYM: poison

Notes Although *antidote* is narrowly used for something that counteracts a poison or toxin, it can also be used in a more general sense to mean anything that solves a problem: "The *antidote* to world hunger is quite simply to feed everyone."

Exploit [verb or noun]

as verb

DEFINITION: to take advantage of

To defeat you in jujitsu, I will **exploit** your every weakness, including your lack of consciousness.

SYNONYMS: use, employ
ANTONYMS: waste, leave unused

as noun

DEFINITION: an adventure or heroic act

I, mighty Hercules, have accomplished many heroic feats! Poets the world over tell of my **exploits** in song! And yet I still can't get the hang of fractions. What the blazes is a numerator?

SYNONYMS: feat, deed

Notes The word can be neutral or it can have negative connotations. *Exploiting* a person often means misusing them for your own purposes. But *exploitation* of a natural resource, for example, may mean that you're simply using it. Still, *exploitive* behavior can lead to overuse and abuse, both of people and of things.

Deride [verb]

DEFINITION: to insult or ridicule

Children will often **deride** others because they're different, which is why there was rarely any peace for Phillip, who was actually half boy, half squid.

SYNONYMS: jeer, humiliate
ANTONYMS: praise, **extol**

Notes   Watch for the noun *derision* or the adjective *derisive*: "Phillip suffered their *derision* silently for years, but finally shot back with a *derisive* 'Eat my ink...vertebrates!'"

Esoteric [adjective]

DEFINITION: known only by a select few

Quincy sought the **esoteric** knowledge held by the Girl Scouts, but wearing the uniform and hocking cookies did nothing to bring their ancient secrets to light.

SYNONYMS: **obscure**, arcane
ANTONYMS: famous, well-known

Notes   *Esoteric* carries the meaning of both "confidential" and "difficult to understand." So even if Quincy were granted access to the Girl Scouts' *esoteric* knowledge, he still might not be able to understand it.

Melancholy [adjective or noun]

DEFINITION: sad or depressed

Rainy days used to make me **melancholy**; then I found Grandpa's stash of old swimsuit calendars.

SYNONYMS: sorrowful, despondent
ANTONYMS: happy, cheerful

Notes   People are *melancholy*. Things or situations that inspire *melancholy* are *melancholic*: "The senior prom song, 'Life is Joyless,' while unusually *melancholic*, nonetheless had a snappy beat."

Rarely you will find this word in its noun form: "King Lügeschnitzel soothed his *melancholy* by watching the funny, dancing monkey."

Ironic [*adjective*]

describing the difference between expectation and reality

It's **ironic** that the Titanic was called the "unsinkable ship," because that sucker went down like a fat man on a seesaw.

SYNONYMS: contrary, incongruous
ANTONYMS: appropriate, expected

Notes Ah yes: the mother of all misused words. Some examples of what it DOESN'T mean:

"Oh yeah, right. Like I really want to take the SAT. Duh!" This is sarcasm, not *irony*.

"I busted my butt to study for the SAT, but on the day of the test, I got sick!" This is an unlucky coincidence, but it's not *irony*.

"Chad was so arrogant, bragging to everyone about how well he was going to do, and then he tanked the test!" This is poetic justice, not *irony*.

Here's what *irony* really is:

"I am a full professor of English at Yale, I have a functional vocabulary of nearly 400,000 words, and yet I was stumped by the SAT sentence completions." We'd expect an English professor to ace the SAT sentence completions, and yet he did not. THAT's *ironic*!

Inhibition [*noun*]

something that prevents or restricts

I'm afraid to go outside, I can't stand to be touched, and I despise laughter—three **inhibitions** that help me live life to its emptiest.

SYNONYMS: hang-up, limitation

Notes *Inhibition* and the very similar word *prohibition* are often used interchangeably, but there's a slight difference. A *prohibition* suggests some outside authority that prevents you, while an *inhibition* is often an inner obstacle, such as a sense of guilt or shame, that restricts you.

The adjective forms *inhibited* and *prohibited* also differ along these lines. If you are *inhibited*, you may feel emotionally blocked. If you're *prohibited*, there's probably some kind of rule blocking you.

Jargon [*noun*]

DEFINITION: vocabulary understood by a specific group of people

The doctors discussed Verne's injuries in such complex medical **jargon** that all he got from their conversation was that he was toast.

SYNONYM: terminology
ANTONYMS: vernacular, layman's terms

Notes *Jargon* can also mean any language that is impossible to understand, or babble, though this meaning is less common than the one relating to technical or specialized vocabulary.

Gullible [*adjective*]

DEFINITION: easily misled or cheated

My little sister is so **gullible**, she thinks the tooth fairy comes to collect her lost teeth, but we know it's really Grandpa who swipes them for his dentures.

SYNONYMS: credulous, naïve
ANTONYMS: skeptical, **incredulous**

Notes The word comes from the noun *gull* (no, not the seabird), which means "a person who is easily deceived." The noun form, *gullibility*, is a likely contender for an appearance on the SAT.

Verify [*verb*]

DEFINITION: to confirm the accuracy of something

Though instant replay **verified** the referee's call, the rowdy Jets fans bombarded him with batteries anyway.

SYNONYMS: prove, authenticate
ANTONYMS: disprove, invalidate

Notes This word comes from the Latin *veritas*, which means "truth." We get a lot of A-list words from the prefix, like *veritable*, *verisimilitude* (one of our faves), and even *very*.

See *verifiable* in "Somnambulist" for more jaw-dropping information.

Volition [noun]

DEFINITION: conscious will, choice

I went to the Nepalese restaurant of my own **volition**, but I had to be forced to try the yak bladder pudding.

SYNONYM: determination
ANTONYM: unwillingness

Notes   *Volition* is often used to point out that nothing forced us to act. We made a conscious choice to go to the restaurant, but no force on earth could make us *want* to try yak bladder pudding (though it is said to be quite the delicacy in Kathmandu).

Emerge [verb]

DEFINITION: to come out from

When surfers drop into the tube on a heavy wave, they'll either **emerge** on the other side in a spray of white water, or they'll be crushed to a paste on the reefs below.

SYNONYMS: manifest, appear
ANTONYMS: withdraw, merge

Notes   The adjective form *emergent* gives us one of our most useful nouns, *emergency*. Think of something suddenly happening, something "coming out" of normal existence (usually bad) that demands our immediate attention. That's an *emergency*.

LYRIC FREAKS!

Directions: Fill in the blanks with a word (or words) from the lyrics.

1. Love has been so _____ to me,
   it's caused me harm and tension

   a. gullible
   b. esoteric
   c. melancholy
   d. injurious
   e. elusive

2. I might be so gullible I'll _____

   a. express my grief to you
   b. laugh at an inappropriate time
   c. rescue you from sorrow
   d. take advantage of you
   e. believe in anything and everything

3. I may not speak your language

   Don't know your _____

   a. jargon
   b. blueprint
   c. exploitations
   d. inhibition
   e. adulation

4. Try not to insult or _____ me

   a. exploit
   b. verify
   c. terminate
   d. deride
   e. heed

5. There's no time for inhibition

   _____

   a. Don't hold back your emotions
   b. Don't be lazy at this moment
   c. Don't be careless with emotions
   d. Don't be bold with your emotions
   e. Don't be timid at this moment

PLUG IN!

Directions: Draw lines to match each word on the left to the correct definition on the right.

1. Elusive
2. Blueprint
3. Yearning
4. Lamentation
5. Injurious
6. Premonition
7. Lofty
8. Heed
9. Adulation
10. Terminate
11. Panacea
12. Antidote
13. Exploit
14. Deride
15. Esoteric
16. Melancholy
17. Ironic
18. Inhibition
19. Jargon
20. Gullible
21. Verify
22. Volition
23. Emerge

a. High, noble
b. Harmful
c. Praise, admiration
d. Cure-all
e. Take advantage of
f. Sad, depressed, blue
g. Expression of grief or sorrow
h. Sense of things to come
i. Prove
j. To come out from
k. Insult
l. Difficult to capture
m. Something that restricts or holds back
n. Naïve, easily misled
o. Describing the difference between expectation and reality
p. To end
q. Detailed plan
r. Pay attention to
s. Specialized vocabulary
t. Known only by a select few
u. Something that relieves or reverses
v. Longing, craving
w. Choice, conscious will

AMP IT UP!

Directions: Fill in the blanks, using the word (or words) that best completes the meaning of the sentence.

1. I'm not saying I can foresee the future, but I had a _____ that something like this might happen.

a. yearning
b. premonition
c. blueprint
d. dream
e. verification

2. To complete the assignment, use all available resources; don't be afraid to _____ your teachers, friends, and textbooks.

a. verify
b. terminate
c. heed
d. exploit
e. emerge

3. If Einstein's theories weren't so _____ and obscure, I'd be able to better understand today's physics lecture.

a. esoteric
b. elusive
c. misunderstood
d. common
e. gullible

4. Most scholars _____ for the Nobel Prize, but no matter how strong their desire, very few will ever earn it.

a. emerge
b. elude
c. yearn
d. verify
e. contend

5. The funeral's mood was appropriately _____, as everyone expressed their grief through _____.

a. gloomy—inhibition
b. hopeful—irony
c. melancholy—lamentation
d. injurious—jargon
e. ironic—yearning

ANSWER KEY

Lyric Freaks!

1) d; 2) e; 3) a; 4) d; 5) a

Plug In!

1) l; 2) q; 3) v; 4) g; 5) b; 6) h; 7) a;
8) r; 9) c; 10) p; 11) d; 12) u; 13) e;
14) k; 15) t; 16) f; 17) o; 18) m; 19) s;
20) n; 21) i; 22) w; 23) j

Amp It Up!

1. b

All you need for this one is a synonym for the keywords *foresee the future*, and there's only one here: *premonition* (*But I've a premonition, a feeling something soon may happen*). Of course, you've gotta know what it means if you're gonna get the right answer.

2. d

The keywords here? *Use all available resources.* That means you need a word closely resembling that phrase, and the only one is *exploit* (*Don't exploit my weakness/Don't you take advantage of me*).

3. a

The keyword here is *obscure*, and the answer choice closest in meaning to *obscure* is *esoteric* (*Love is only known by a chosen few, it seems so esoteric*).

4. c

Yup, they all want that Nobel Prize. Many of these answer choices seem like possibilities, but we're looking for the one that most closely shares a meaning with the keyword, *desire*. The only one that works is *yearn* (*Don't you know I'm yearning/Longing for your eyes on me*).

5. c

Most funerals are depressing affairs; so right off the bat only choices a and c, *gloomy* and *melancholy*, make sense in the first blank (*It makes me melancholy and blue, if that's love then how ironic*). As far as the next blank goes, we need a word that means "expressing grief," and *lamentation* is precisely that (*Hear my lamentation/It's the expression of my grief*).

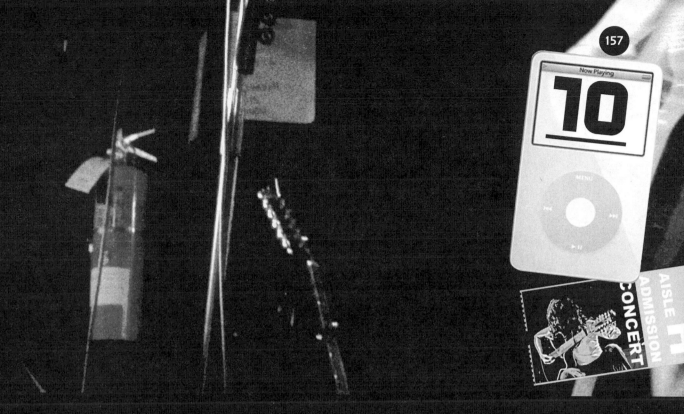

AISLE
ADMISSION
CONCERT

PROMONTORY

Promontory

We're on a **promontory**
High above the sea
Reminisce with me
Think back on how we came to be
Like this, so **amorphous**
We're so shapeless and unformed
We're gonna waste away into nothing, baby

You know that you're the queen
The **monarch**, you're supreme
Infallible, you can do no wrong
So why you stringing me along
I try to tell you this, but like a **plagiarist**
You steal my words away
And I forget just what I had to say

And I've been **ravenous** and **rapacious** too
I hunger for you, yes I do
Indelible, I can't be removed
No matter what you put me through
I just can't compete when it comes to you

Our total love's a **meager** sum
A **paucity**, it's next to none
Don't **repudiate** me, don't discard me
Your neglect has really **marred** me
It's damaged me, done harm to me
We've got to turn ourselves around
Got to work our way back to solid ground

And I've been **ravenous** and **rapacious** too
I hunger for you, yes I do
Indelible, I can't be removed
No matter what you put me through
I just can't compete when it comes to you
Yeah, I'm just some kind of fool when it comes to you

Our love was **comprehensive** when we started
It was all-inclusive
Now it seems to me that we've **plateaued**
There's no growth
Have I worn out my **utility**
I'm not useful anymore
Now it's all **sobriety**
But we were never this serious before

On a **promontory**
High above the sea
Don't you push me
We can **reconcile** and be
Together again, best of friends
This **rivalry** is through
I just can't compete when it comes to you

And I've been **ravenous** and **rapacious** too
I hunger for you, yes I do
Indelible, I can't be removed
No matter what you put me through
I just can't compete when it comes to you
Yeah, I'm just some kind of fool when it comes to you
Yeah, yeah, I don't know what I'm gonna do when it comes to you
We're on a **promontory**

Promontory [noun]

DEFINITION: an overhanging, elevated place

Standing high on the **promontory** above the African plains, Marcia and Sam gazed into each other's eyes and decided that what they each desired most was to push the other off.

SYNONYMS: ledge, precipice

Notes If you think of the word *prominent* (see "Somnambulist"), which describes anything that sticks out, you'll be getting close to *promontory*. A *promontory* sticks out into space.

Reminisce [verb]

DEFINITION: to recall the past

As Egbert **reminisced** sweetly about the happy times he'd shared with Leslie in kindergarten this year, she super-glued his nostrils shut.

SYNONYMS: remember, reflect
ANTONYM: forget

Notes *Reminisce* has a slightly different meaning than *remember*. *Reminiscing* takes a while as you replay scenes and events in your head. It also carries the sense that the memories were happy ones, whereas *remember* is neutral.

The adjective *reminiscent* has a slightly different meaning. If something's *reminiscent*, it reminds you of something else: "The flavor of your tuna casserole is slightly *reminiscent* of my grandma's ear medicine, but not nearly as tasty."

Amorphous [*adjective*]

DEFINITION: without definite shape

Shane's worst fears were realized when the **amorphous** glob of ooze he'd found in his basement demanded a huge batch of Jell-O to serve as its mate.

SYNONYMS: formless, protean
ANTONYM: well-defined

Notes   The prefix *a-* means "without"; the suffix *-morph* means "shape."

Individual things can be *amorphous*, like clouds, amoebas, or globs of ooze, but large groups of things can also lack definite shape, as an *amorphous* crowd or *amorphous* herd of wildebeest.

Monarch [*noun*]

DEFINITION: a supreme ruler

King Lügeschnitzel was thought of as a gentle **monarch** because he had peasants tortured for his amusement only during midafternoon strüdel.

SYNONYMS: lord, sovereign
ANTONYMS: serf, commoner

Notes   *Monarchs* are usually the big kahuna—kings and queens. Dukes, earls, counts, viscounts, lords, and all the lesser stars in the sky aren't considered *monarchs*.

A nation ruled by kings and queens is called a *monarchy*. A few of them still exist. However, most royalty have no real political power; they just tool around in limos trying to avoid tabloid photographers.

Infallible [*adjective*]

DEFINITION: unable to make a mistake

This ointment is an **infallible** remedy for your foot fungus; it will either kill the fungus or liquefy your foot. Either way, no fungus!

SYNONYMS: unerring, perfect
ANTONYMS: fallible, flawed

> **Notes** If you get stuck, use this workaround: if something's *in-fall-ible*, it cannot "fall."

Plagiarist [*noun*]

DEFINITION: a person who steals another's ideas or writings

Just copy my paper already; you'll be a **plagiarist**, but at least people won't know you're as dumb as a toaster.

SYNONYM: copycat
ANTONYM: author

> **Notes** After three years of high school English you all should know how to *plagiarize* pretty well by now. You also probably know that it's really hard to get away with *plagiarism*, even if you tweak the original text file you downloaded from the Web.

Ravenous [*adjective*]

DEFINITION: extremely hungry

Joanie was **ravenous** after spending the weekend locked in the biology lab; we found her on Monday morning chowing a cricket specimen. "Cruuuuunchy," she drooled.

SYNONYMS: starving, **voracious**
ANTONYMS: **satiated**, full

> **Notes** Although the raven—the big, hungry black bird—is not related to *ravenous*, you can still use it to remember, since ravens are always hungry. We never met a raven who wouldn't peck out your eyes for a quick snack.

Rapacious [*adjective*]

DEFINITION: excessively greedy or hungry

Few animals rival the shark in its **rapacious** pursuit of food; it eats everything it can smell, including happy little children floating in their inner tubes.

SYNONYMS: voracious, **ravenous**
ANTONYM: sated

> **Notes** It's no accident that the word shares a root with *rape*; *rapacity* means a violent, aggressive kind of hunger—the kind a Viking might have had after a month at sea.
>
> *Rapacity* can indicate hunger for food, but it can also mean a hunger for anything that satisfies a particular desire.

Indelible [*adjective*]

DEFINITION: impossible to remove

Helga wished she hadn't used **indelible** ink to scrawl "You're all a bunch of gübers" in the boys' bathroom, because she'd misspelled "goobers" and now couldn't correct it.

SYNONYMS: permanent, ineffaceable
ANTONYMS: erasable, **ephemeral**

> **Notes** Physical things can have *indelibility*, like the permanent ink in the sentence above, but ideas, sensations, and memories can also be described as *indelible*: "I can't forget the *indelible* memory of graduation, especially since it happened five minutes ago."

Meager [*adjective*]

DEFINITION: of little value or quantity

Mitchell's **meager** salary would never allow him to date the supermodel he'd been lusting after because he couldn't support her $12,000-a-day bottled water habit.

SYNONYMS: insufficient, inadequate
ANTONYMS: rich, abundant

Paucity [*noun*]

DEFINITION: a small amount or number

Given the **paucity** of women willing to date a portable toilet cleaner guy, Mitchell contented himself with late night TV, his dog Fred, and his vast collection of plungers.

SYNONYMS: dearth, scarcity
ANTONYMS: wealth, plenty

Notes You might notice that the word shares a root with *pauper*, which means "a very poor person."

Paucity can be used to mean both smallness in number and in quantity, for example, a *paucity* of qualified teachers or a *paucity* of fresh water.

Repudiate [*verb*]

DEFINITION: to reject or cut all ties

When Russia **repudiated** China's offer of a free-trade agreement, officials in Beijing responded by canceling Russia's order of sweet and sour pork.

SYNONYMS: disavow, **renounce**
ANTONYMS: accept, welcome

Notes This word comes from the Latin *repudium*, meaning "divorce." So when you reject your husband or wife enough to divorce them, you're *repudiating* them.

Marred [verb or adjective]

DEFINITION: past tense of *mar*, to spoil the perfection of something

The peaceful beauty of the Buddhist temple was **marred** by the new Admiral Greaseburger franchise across the hall from the meditation room.

SYNONYMS: corrupt, **taint**
ANTONYMS: purify, cleanse

Notes   *Mar* is one of several words that mean "to cause harm." Others are *injure*, *damage*, and *impair*. But only *mar* has the meaning of "spoiling perfection."

Comprehensive [adjective]

DEFINITION: including everything

Well, Jaime, a **comprehensive** list of your faults would take hours to recite, but I'll start with ugly, boring, slow-witted, flea-infested, smelly, turkey-necked...wait, did I say smelly?

SYNONYMS: complete, thorough
ANTONYMS: incomplete, partial

Notes   Be careful, *comprehensive* doesn't mean quite the same thing as the verb, *comprehend*, which means "to understand completely."

Plateaued [verb]

DEFINITION: past tense of *plateau*, to flatten or stabilize after an increase

While my skills as a boxer have definitely **plateaued**, I'm better than ever at acting shocked when the judges declare the other guy the winner.

SYNONYMS: level off, smooth out
ANTONYMS: vary, **oscillate**

Notes   The noun form, *plateau*, means "a high, flat area of land." To get to it, you have to first go uphill, but then it levels off. In the same way, to *plateau* means "to level off after increase or improvement."

Utility [*noun or adjective*]

DEFINITION: usefulness

While in our evolutionary past the human appendix may have had some **utility**, today it serves no purpose but to swell to the size of a pineapple and burst.

SYNONYMS: convenience, applicability
ANTONYM: uselessness

Notes It's helpful to remember the verb form, *utilize*, which means "to use." Thus, anything with *utility* is useful. This can apply to things, like tools, or to ideas: "Architects the world over have recognized the *utility* of the Pythagorean theorem. Without it, all our triangles would be obtuse! OBTUUUUUUUSE!"

As an adjective, *utility* means used or working in several capacities, such as a *utility* cast member or a *utility* infielder.

Sobriety [*noun*]

DEFINITION: serious or calm in manner

Arthur shattered the heavy **sobriety** of the occasion when he danced a clumsy jig on his landlord's fresh grave.

SYNONYMS: solemnity, gravity
ANTONYMS: **frivolity**, silliness

Notes *Sobriety* also means the state of being *sober*; that is, not drunk.

Sober might remind you of the adjective *somber*, but they differ slightly. While *sober* suggests seriousness, *somber* describes something heavy, sad, or **melancholy**.

Reconcile [*verb*]

DEFINITION 1: to restore friendship or harmony

Though I love you dearly, Helen, I doubt we can **reconcile** our differences. I'm a caring, sensitive man, and you're a rampaging highland gorilla.

SYNONYMS: settle, appease
ANTONYMS: argue, differ

DEFINITION 2: to make even

It was always difficult for the accounting team to **reconcile** billionaire Gilbert Worthington III's finances because he stashed most of his money in his Radioactive Vault of Doom.

SYNONYMS: adjust, rectify
ANTONYM: skew

Rivalry [*noun*]

DEFINITION: competition

Years of bitter sibling **rivalry** ended when, at the age of 63, Yvette finally let her brother Ricky have the green clovers in her Lucky Charms.

SYNONYMS: feud, fight
ANTONYM: cooperation

Notes When you remember that a *rival* is an opponent or enemy, it's not a big stretch of logic to figure out what a *rivalry* is. If this is a big stretch, then perhaps a long, fulfilling career in fast-food preparation is in store for you.

LYRIC FREAKS!

Directions: Fill in the blanks with a word (or words) from the lyrics.

1. You know that you're the queen

The _____, you're supreme

a. promontory
b. rivalry
c. monarch
d. plagiarist
e. plateau

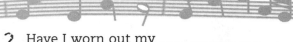

2. Have I worn out my _____

I'm not useful anymore

a. utility
b. rivalry
c. promontory
d. sobriety
e. paucity

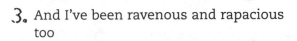

3. And I've been ravenous and rapacious too

_____, yes I do

a. I live to serve you
b. I care about you
c. I've got spirit
d. I daydream about you
e. I hunger for you

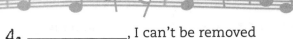

4. _____, I can't be removed

No matter what you put me through

a. Comprehensive
b. Indelible
c. Amorphous
d. Infallible
e. Ravenous

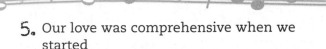

5. Our love was comprehensive when we started

It was _____

a. all-intrusive
b. all-elusive
c. all-exclusive
d. all-abusive
e. all-inclusive

PLUG IN!

Directions: Draw lines to match each word (or words) on the left to the correct definition on the right.

1 Promontory	a. Serious or calm manner
2 Reminisce	b. Supreme ruler
3 Amorphous	c. Of little value or quantity
4 Monarch	d. One who steals another's words or ideas
5 Plagiarist	e. Competition
6 Ravenous, Rapacious	f. Shapeless, unformed
7 Indelible	g. Impossible to remove, unforgettable
8 Meager	h. To restore friendship
9 Paucity	i. Flatten out, to show no growth
10 Repudiate	j. Usefulness
11 Marred	k. Overhanging, elevated place
12 Comprehensive	l. To reject, discard
13 Plateau	m. Spoiled, damaged
14 Utility	n. Scarcity
15 Sobriety	o. Think back, recall the past
16 Reconcile	p. Extremely hungry
17 Rivalry	q. All-inclusive, complete

AMP IT UP!

Directions: Fill in the blanks, choosing the word (or words) that best completes the meaning of the sentence.

1. When the teacher discovers that you've copied my paper, you'll be expelled from school for _____.

    a. cheating
    b. dishonesty
    c. plagiarism
    d. sobriety
    e. paucity

2. Seeing the pizza commercial on television _____ John's already _____ appetite.

    a. reduced–large
    b. marred–rapacious
    c. magnified–meager
    d. increased–ravenous
    e. removed–voracious

3. Every Opening Day, my grandfather meets his childhood friends at Yankee Stadium, where they _____ about old times over a ballgame.

    a. reminisce
    b. repudiate
    c. reconcile
    d. plagiarize
    e. communicate

4. Because of the _____ of food and fresh water in the desert, the creatures that live there must survive on a _____ diet.

    a. scarcity–luxurious
    b. frequency–sober
    c. inadequacy–comprehensive
    d. utility–varied
    e. paucity–meager

5. Our experience of watching the beautiful sunset was _____ by the arrival of a noisy group of tourists.

    a. reconciled
    b. marred
    c. ruined
    d. repudiated
    e. utilized

ANSWER KEY

Lyric Freaks!

1) c; 2) a; 3) e; 4) b; 5) e

Plug In!

1) k; 2) o; 3) f; 4) b; 5) d; 6) p; 7) g;
8) c; 9) n; 10) l; 11) m; 12) q; 13) i;
14) j; 15) a; 16) h; 17) e

Amp It Up!

1. c

Choices a, b, and c are all things for which you could get expelled, but only one accurately describes the crime of stealing another person's writing: *plagiarism* (*I try to tell you this, but like a plagiarist/You steal my words away*).

2. d

John's got a pretty big appetite to begin with, and the commercial only made it worse. This one's difficult because there are so many words that could work well in the second blank—*rapacious, ravenous* (*And I've been ravenous and rapacious too/I hunger for you, yes I do*) and, if you're really good, *voracious*, another synonym for *ravenous*. Likewise, there are a couple of choices that could work in the first blank, like *increased* or *magnified*. But only one pair works for both: choice d.

3. a

Reminisce is the best choice for this sentence (*Reminisce with me/Think back on what we came to be*). *Reconcile*, which means "to restore friendship or harmony," is interesting but there's nothing in the sentence that suggests the friendships were ever broken (*We can reconcile and be/Together again, best of friends*). *Communicate* seems like a close fit, but it's not as specific as *reminisce*, which means "to think about or discuss past experiences."

4. e

For the first blank, choices a, c, and e would all make sense because they are synonyms for "a lack of." The only logical word for the second blank, though, is *meager*, because the sentence suggests that creatures don't have a lot of food in the desert (*Our total love's a meager sum/A paucity, it's next to none*).

5. b

The tourists' arrival has brought our author down when he was trying to enjoy the sunset. Therefore, either *marred* or *ruined* seems correct. In this case, *marred* is a better choice because we cannot assume that the people watching the sunset got absolutely no pleasure out of it. *Ruin* is an absolute word, while *mar* is less complete (*Your neglect has really marred me/It's damaged me, done harm to me*). As a rule, go with the less absolute choice.

Now Playing

11

THE REAL ME

The Real Me

I'm **abstruse**, I'm **obscure**
A mystery for sure, you don't know me
You're a **dupe**, you're a fool
To think you love me like you do, you don't know me
You don't know me

You know what I would do
I would **taint** and soil you
That's just what I'd do

It's **innate**, it's **inborn**
It's just the way I'm formed, I'm just nasty
I'll **recant**, take it back
And then stab you in the back, you can't trust me
No you can't trust me

Well I can look you in the eye
As I **slander** and I lie
Look me in the eye

And see the real me
Condemn and disapprove of me
I'm not worthy of imitation
I'm not **exemplary**
Cruelty's my **proficiency**
It's something I do skillfully
So **migrate** like a bird in winter
And fly away from me

You **retort**, answer back
You argue and attack, but I'm not listening
You control, **regulate**
And I just can't relate, no I'm not listening
I'm not listening

I'm narrow in my views
I'm **provincial** and **parochial** too
I don't have room for you

Nullify and **negate**
Wipe me off the slate, just dismiss me
I'll **exploit**, I will use
I'm **unethical**, I'll break all the rules
Dismiss me
Yeah you'd best dismiss me

You won't change who I am
I'm an **indomitable** man
An unconquerable man

So see the real me
Condemn and disapprove of me
I'm not worthy of imitation
I'm not **exemplary**
Cruelty's my **proficiency**
It's something I do skillfully
So **migrate** like a bird in winter
And fly away from me

Abstruse [*adjective*]

DEFINITION: difficult to understand

The physics lab instructions were so **abstruse** that the confused students accidentally opened a space/time rift through which enormous prehistoric mosquitoes swarmed and sucked everyone dry of blood.

SYNONYMS: complex, intricate
ANTONYMS: simple, straightforward

Notes We use *abstruse* in situations when something's hard to understand because it's extremely complicated, like the mathematics of time travel or opening a tamper-proof medicine bottle. If something's hard to understand because it's just confusing or illogical, it's not *abstruse*.

Don't confuse *abstruse* with *abstract*, which has several meanings, one of which is also "difficult to understand," but not because a thing is complicated. *Abstractions* are difficult to understand because they don't have a physical reality; they're just ideas or concepts.

Obscure [*adjective or verb*]

as adjective

DEFINITION 1: not clearly seen or understood

When the archeologists finally translated the **obscure** symbols on the mummy's tomb, they were shocked to find it read: "For a good time, call Nefertiti."

SYNONYMS: cryptic, mysterious
ANTONYMS: clear, intelligible

DEFINITION 2: little-known

Thanks to an **obscure** clause in your cell phone contract, MegaCorpCom, Inc. (a subsidiary of UltraMegaCorpCom, Inc.) now owns both your lungs. Should have read the fine print, eh? Out with them, then.

SYNONYMS: hidden, buried
ANTONYMS: famous, well-known

as verb

DEFINITION: to hide or conceal

Though a baseball cap hid his bald spot, there was simply no garment on earth that could **obscure** Kenneth's massive bat-like wings.

SYNONYMS: mask, cover up
ANTONYM: reveal

Dupe [*noun*]

DEFINITION: a fool

Always the **dupe** of her brother's practical jokes, Gretchen once again found herself smeared with meat sauce and trapped in the tiger cage.

SYNONYMS: victim, sucker

Notes See "Duped Again" to check out the verb form of *dupe*.

Taint [*verb*]

DEFINITION: to soil or contaminate

You've once again **tainted** my movie experience by hogging the popcorn, giving away the ending, and repeatedly screaming "Fire!"

SYNONYMS: pollute, **mar**
ANTONYMS: purify, cleanse

Notes If you're reminded of *stain* or *paint*, then you're on the right track. Both mean "to change color," and share the same root with *taint*. Just remember that, like *stain*, a *taint* puts a negative mark on something otherwise positive.

Innate [*adjective*]

DEFINITION: instinctual, not learned

While the desire to eat is **innate**, the desire to eat tofu must be learned.

SYNONYMS: **inborn**, inherent
ANTONYMS: learned, acquired

Inborn [*adjective*]

DEFINITION: existing at birth

Vesuvio had an **inborn** understanding of physics; by the age of five, he had designed an antiballistic missile system for his tree house.

SYNONYMS: **innate**, instinctual
ANTONYM: learned

Notes Basically, humans are born knowing how to do a few things. Not many, of course, but breathing, pooping, and sucking are pretty much *innate* and *inborn* drives.

There's some debate about whether specific talents, like musical, mathematical, or language skills have some basis in *innate* characteristics that develop into astonishing abilities. Like those annoying children who at four years old are better at playing the violin than you will be at anything in your life, ever.

Recant [*verb*]

DEFINITION: to take back a statement

Galileo's lesser-known brother, Gary, was forced to **recant** his astronomical findings publicly, but in private he still maintained that the sun was, in fact, an all-powerful, flaming monkey.

SYNONYMS: **renounce**, withdraw
ANTONYMS: stand by, uphold

Slander [*verb or noun*]

DEFINITION: to make damaging but false statements about a person

Why must you **slander** me, Grandma; I've never even *seen* a ferret, much less trained one to steal your medication.

SYNONYMS: defame, malign
ANTONYMS: **extol**, compliment

Notes   For something to count as *slander* (the noun form), it has to be a knowingly false statement. Simply insulting someone is not *slander*. Lying about someone to damage their reputation, however, is *slanderous*.

Condemn [*verb*]

DEFINITION: to damn or judge negatively

Though the judge **condemned** Virgil for his terrible crimes, she also praised his lovely personal aroma.

SYNONYMS: **denounce**, reproach
ANTONYMS: praise, commend

Notes   People who have done something evil or wrong deserve *condemnation*. The word can also be used more narrowly to mean "to judge unfit," as in to *condemn* an old building that's in danger of collapse.

Exemplary [*adjective*]

DEFINITION: worthy of imitation

Despite my **exemplary** performance on the SAT, I'm still unemployed, frightened, and so very, very lonely.

SYNONYMS: commendable, **laudable**
ANTONYM: regrettable

Notes Usually, *exemplary* is used to describe a positive example, one you'd encourage others to follow. Sometimes, however, it can be neutral, describing something that serves as an illustration.

The noun form, *exemplar*, is a person or thing that sets the example to follow.

Proficiency [*noun*]

DEFINITION: a skill or capability

Margaret's greatest **proficiency** is translating languages, but surely she goofed when she said the Swedish ambassador requested a "fat rubber dumpling" at the summit.

SYNONYMS: expertise, ability
ANTONYMS: deficiency, incompetence

Notes Remember it this way: if you're *proficient* at something, you're a *pro*. Yes, yes, we know *pro* is short for *professional*, but let's not split hairs, shall we?

Migrate [verb]

DEFINITION: to move from one place to another

During the winter months, millions of Canada geese **migrate** to warmer regions, where they soil lawns and golf courses with puddles of oozy goose-poop.

SYNONYMS: travel, move
ANTONYM: stay put

Notes *Migration* usually refers to movement over long distances for long periods of time. *Migrants* tend to go from one place to another in a single direction, rather than just moving around or traveling randomly.

The related word, *emigrate*, has a slightly different meaning. Whereas *migrants* may eventually return to where they came from, as some birds do each year, *emigrants* usually move to a new place to live permanently. This is closer in meaning to *immigrate*, which means to enter a place and establish yourself there.

But, forgetting all those fine points, if you can just remember that all three, *migrate*, *emigrate*, and *immigrate* have something to do with moving from one place to another, you'll be alllll-right.

Retort [verb or noun]

DEFINITION: to answer back

After Jill shouted "I know you are, but what am I?" for the nineteenth time, Michael finally **retorted**, "Shut up. Please shut up. For the love of all things holy, won't you shut up!"

SYNONYMS: counter, rebut
ANTONYM: remain silent

Notes You can *retort* sharply, as in the above sentence, or you can simply respond to a statement, as you might in the counterargument of a debate.

As a noun, a *retort* is a reply to an insult or argument, often **witty** or cutting.

Regulate [verb]

DEFINITION: to control or direct

If the government really wants to **regulate** teen smoking, all it needs to do is eliminate teens. Problem solved!

SYNONYMS: direct, govern
ANTONYMS: liberate, free

Notes *Regulate* shares a root with *regular*, which as you already know means "standard" or "ordered." That's what *regulations* do: maintain standards and order. Boring, but necessary.

Provincial [adjective or noun]

DEFINITION: narrow-minded

Call me **provincial**, but I think anything I don't like should be illegal.

SYNONYMS: unaware, ignorant
ANTONYMS: worldly, cosmopolitan

Notes As a noun, a *provincial* is someone from the countryside. As an adjective, however, it means "narrow-minded" or "lacking in refinement." As anyone from the country can tell you, people out there are often no less ignorant and narrow-minded than city-folk, but the fact that *provincial* has come to have such a negative meaning is good evidence that, historically, the people who write dictionaries live in cities.

Parochial [*adjective*]

DEFINITION: narrow or limited in scope

Ewan wondered why his parents had such a **parochial** attitude about fashion; he thought he looked fabulous in a sundress and pumps.

SYNONYMS: **provincial**, ignorant
ANTONYMS: sophisticated, open-minded

Notes Like *provincial*, *parochial* suggests closed-mindedness or limited knowledge, but it doesn't carry with it the sense of someone being dumb because they're from the boonies. More accurately, it means that a person has a specific way of seeing the world and can't go beyond his or her own frame of understanding to grasp a wider view.

Nullify [*verb*]

DEFINITION: to render powerless

If we hope to defeat the invading aliens, we must first **nullify** their ability to destroy all humanity with a single thought. Well...any suggestions?

SYNONYMS: annul, **negate**
ANTONYMS: empower, enable

Notes The word *null* means nothing, zip, zero, none, zilch. If you *nullify* something, you reduce it to just that: nothing.

Similar words include *nullity* (nothingness), *annul* (reduce to nothing, neutralize), and *nil* (nothing). That we have so many words to mean nothing must mean something.

Negate [*verb*]

DEFINITION: to cancel out

Marquesha **negated** Joe-Bob's good mood by telling him he smelled like "bad fish."

SYNONYMS: **nullify**, invalidate
ANTONYMS: affirm, validate

Notes No doubt you've already noticed this word's similarity to *negative*, its adjective form. The noun is *negation*.

Exploit [*verb or noun*]

as verb

DEFINITION: to take advantage of

To defeat you in jujitsu, I will **exploit** your every weakness, including your lack of consciousness.

SYNONYMS: use, employ
ANTONYMS: waste, leave unused

as noun

DEFINITION: an adventure or heroic act

I, mighty Hercules, have accomplished many heroic feats! Poets the world over tell of my **exploits** in song! And yet I still can't get the hang of fractions. What the blazes is a numerator?

SYNONYMS: feat, deed

Notes See "Imagination" for more mind-blowing information. We liked this word so much, we had to use it again.

Unethical [adjective]

DEFINITION: unjust in action or behavior

While some considered it **unethical** for Principal Schatz to date the lunch lady, most just thought it was nasty.

SYNONYMS: dishonorable, immoral
ANTONYMS: ethical, moral

Notes *Ethics* is the branch of philosophy that studies moral values; that is, what's right and what's wrong. After centuries of careful thought, the conclusion seems to be this: *ethical* behavior is being nice to people and *unethical* behavior is being naughty.

Indomitable [adjective]

DEFINITION: unconquerable or invincible

I, Siegfried the **Indomitable** and Very Naughty Warrior of the North, will seize your lands and enslave your people…uh…if that's okay with you.

SYNONYMS: insurmountable, unbeatable
ANTONYMS: weak, feeble

Notes This word derives from *dominate*, "to conquer." If you're *domitable*, you can be easily conquered. If you add the negative qualifier *in-*, then you can't be *dominated*. You're *indomitable*. Good for you. Now go kick some butt.

LYRIC FREAKS!

Directions: Fill in the blanks with a word (or words) from the lyrics.

1. Well I can look you in the eye

As I _____ and I lie

Look me in the eye

   a. slander
   b. negate
   c. retort
   d. dupe
   e. nullify

2. I'm narrow in my views

I'm _____ and _____ too

I don't have room for you

   a. exemplary–unethical
   b. proficient–exemplary
   c. abstruse–obscure
   d. innate–inborn
   e. provincial–parochial

3. And see the real me

Condemn and _____

   a. expose the demons in me
   b. be afraid of me
   c. disapprove of me
   d. keep away from me
   e. embrace the bad in me

4. Cruelty's my proficiency

It's something _____

   a. I do constantly
   b. I do willfully
   c. I do happily
   d. I do painfully
   e. I do skillfully

5. I'm _____ I'm _____

A mystery for sure, you don't know me

   a. exemplary–unethical
   b. abstruse–obscure
   c. proficient–exemplary
   d. innate–inborn
   e. provincial–parochial

PLUG IN!

Directions: Draw lines to match each word (or words) on the left to the correct definition on the right.

1. Abstruse, Obscure

2. Dupe

3. Taint

4. Innate, Inborn

5. Recant

6. Slander

7. Condemn

8. Exemplary

9. Proficiency

10. Migrate

11. Retort

12. Regulate

13. Provincial, Parochial

14. Nullify, Negate

15. Exploit

16. Unethical

17. Indomitable

a. To use or take advantage of

b. Difficult to understand, mysterious

c. Narrow in view

d. Unjust, dishonorable, immoral

e. Unconquerable, invincible

f. To move from one place to another

g. To lie, usually in a damaging way

h. To control or direct

i. To cancel out

j. Not learned, existing at birth

k. Fool

l. Skill

m. Worthy of imitation

n. Take back a statement

o. Disapprove, judge negatively

p. To soil or contaminate

q. Answer back

AMP IT UP!

Directions: Fill in the blanks, choosing the word (or words) that best completes the meaning of the sentence.

1. The judge _____ John's repeated acts of petty thievery, and sentenced him to 60 days in prison.

   a. slandered
   b. negated
   c. retorted
   d. explained
   e. condemned

2. For most animals, caring for their young is _____ and instinctual. Unfortunately, humans have no such _____ knowledge and must learn from their parents.

   a. proficient—untainted
   b. abstruse—obscure
   c. proper—appropriate
   d. useful—ready
   e. inborn—innate

3. Alexander the Great was a(n) _____ ruler, defeating all opposition and conquering most of the known world by the time he was 25.

   a. parochial
   b. unethical
   c. indomitable
   d. exemplary
   e. innate

4. My computer crashed at 4 a.m., wiping out every open file and completely _____ five hours' worth of work on my term paper.

   a. upending
   b. negating
   c. obscuring
   d. exploiting
   e. tainting

5. During the televised debate, the Republican candidate began to _____ his Democratic rival, who struggled to _____ his opponent's obvious lies.

   a. condemn—dupe
   b. exploit—remark
   c. nullify—recant
   d. attack—insult
   e. slander—retort

ANSWER KEY

Lyric Freaks!

1) a; 2) e; 3) c; 4) e; 5) b

Plug In!

1) b; 2) k; 3) p; 4) j; 5) n; 6) g; 7) o;
8) m; 9) l; 10) f; 11) q; 12) h; 13) c;
14) i; 15) a; 16) d; 17) e

Amp It Up!

1. e

We know that by sentencing him to jail, the judge definitely disapproved of this thief, so *condemn* is your best bet (*So see the real me/Condemn and disapprove of me*). *Slander* may seem tempting (*I can look you in the eye/As I slander and I lie*), but the judge wasn't lying.

2. e

The first blank has to mean something similar to the keyword *instinctual*, so we can get rid of everything except choice e right away. The word for the second blank should be synonymous with that of the first, and *innate* and *inborn* are synonyms (*It's innate, it's inborn/It's just the way I'm formed*).

3. c

Although he may have been *unethical*, he may have been *parochial*, he may have been an *exemplary* model for other rulers to follow, and he may have had an *innate* knowledge of ruling, the sentence only indicates that Alexander was good at conquering and not getting conquered in return. Therefore, we've got to go with *indomitable* (*I'm an indomitable man/An unconquerable man*).

4. b

This one might warrant a second look because all the answer choices seem to have the same kind of general feeling about them. However, only *negating* means that the work was wiped out by the computer glitch (*Nullify and negate/Wipe me off the slate*).

5. e

Here, the Republican candidate was spreading lies about his Democratic rival. *Slander* means just that, "to spread lies about another" (*Well I can look you in the eye/As I slander and I lie*). The Democratic candidate then struggled to answer, or *retort*, his opponent's false charges (*You retort, answer back*). Choice d is close, but it's not quite as strong as choice e because thinking of a *retort* to someone's lies makes more sense than thinking of an *insult* to someone's lies.

Now Playing

AISLE
ADMISSION
CONCERT

FRUGAL WITH
YOUR LOVE

Frugal with Your Love

Let me tell an **anecdote**, a funny tale
About two people opposed in nature,
   incompatible
You think that I'm **inconsequential**,
   unimportant, just an orphan
When you gonna come around
Show some **compassion** towards
   me, sympathy for me

Why can't you be **amicable**
Friendly and agreeable
Why are you so **frugal** with your love
I need your **camaraderie**
Your friendly sociability
But you're so stingy with your love

Why you got to fight me, got to be
   my **antagonist**
When I'm persistent, so hard-work-
   ing, so **assiduous**
You laugh at my attempts, my hard
   work, my **diligence**
When you gonna come around
Be an **asylum** to me, a **sanctuary**

I can only fight **adversity**
The misfortune you throw at me
When you're so **frugal** with your love
I try to be **benevolent**
Friendly, helpful, heaven-sent
And still you're stingy with your love

Your love is **deleterious**, it's harmful
    and destructive
Your love is **enervating**, it makes me
    too tired to speak
And my **exasperation**, irritation, and
    frustration
It's getting old and **hackneyed** and
    it's making me so weak

I'm only looking for **jubilation**
Festive, joyful celebration
And you're so **frugal** with your love
Lord, give me **sagacity**
Shine some wisdom down on me
What can I do when you're stingy
    with your love

Frugal with your love
Stingy with your love
Frugal with your love
Stingy with your love...

Anecdote [noun]

DEFINITION: a short, often amusing story

The kids hated listening to Grandpa's **anecdotes** about the war because he never shut up about the metal plate in his head and, quite frankly, everyone knew he'd never *been* in the war.

SYNONYM: tale

Incompatible [adjective]

DEFINITION: describing two or more things that cannot exist together

Bev and Jan were **incompatible** roommates. Bev was the quiet type, while Jan was into throwing parties where everyone slathered each other in mayonnaise and played rugby.

SYNONYMS: incongruous, conflicting
ANTONYMS: compatible, well-matched

Inconsequential [adjective]

DEFINITION: trivial or unimportant

As long as you have love, money is **inconsequential**. Unless, of course, you also enjoy food and shelter; then you need money.

SYNONYMS: irrelevant, **impertinent**
ANTONYMS: significant, essential

Notes   If something has no *consequences*, then it simply doesn't matter to you. If you get stuck, remember it that way: something *inconsequential* has "no consequence."

Compassion [noun]

DEFINITION: sympathy for the suffering of others, caring

Those who have **compassion** always offer help to the less fortunate. Those who don't have a lot more free time.

SYNONYM: kindness
ANTONYM: **indifference**

Notes Don't let the word *passion* trip you up! *Passion* has a primary meaning of intense suffering or pain. (Yes, it also means "strong emotion" or even "love," but check the dictionary. Those are secondary meanings.) The prefix, *com-* means "together with," so *compassion* means to share in or at least be aware of the suffering of others. The writers of the SAT are betting that you're going to get distracted by the other meanings of *passion* and offer you incorrect answer choices. Don't give 'em the pleasure.

Also implied by *compassion* is a desire to help the person who is suffering.

Amicable [adjective]

DEFINITION: friendly and agreeable

Dudley would have been a lot more **amicable** if we hadn't kidnapped him, painted his body green, and dropped him off at a rest stop in a strange town.

SYNONYMS: neighborly, peaceable
ANTONYMS: hostile, **antagonistic**

Notes You might see a related word, *amity*, meaning friendship: "The warring parties demonstrated their *amity* by exchanging long, lingering kisses at the start of the peace talks."

Another word, *amiable,* means almost the same thing as *amicable.* *Amiable* means "good-natured" or "pleasant" in general, whereas *amicable* means "neighborly" or "friendly toward others."

Frugal [adjective]

DEFINITION: cheap

Billionaire Gilbert Worthington III was so **frugal**, he'd stand in line for hours at a soup kitchen for the homeless rather than grab a can from one of the five supermarkets he owned.

SYNONYMS: thrifty, parsimonious
ANTONYMS: generous, magnanimous

Notes *Frugal* can have the negative sense of "stingy," as in the above sentence, where the billionaire is cheap to the point of being ridiculous. However, it just as often carries the more neutral sense of simply being economical or sparing with resources.

Camaraderie [noun]

DEFINITION: friendship

The **camaraderie** between Ralphie and his beloved hound, Hank, could never be broken—unless Hank got within sniffing range of a sweet-smellin' poodle in heat.

SYNONYMS: fellowship, brotherhood
ANTONYMS: **antagonism**, enmity

Notes We can't resist: this word comes from the Latin word *camera*. WHAAA? you ask. EXPLAIN! you say. Well, *camera* meant "room," or "chamber," (our *bicameral* Congress has two chambers: the House and Senate). In Middle French the word *camarade* was used to mean "a group of people who sleep in one room," or, more simply, "roommates." If you stay with your roommate long enough, you'd better establish some friendly *camaraderie*. If not, you'll make each other miserable.

Antagonist [*noun*]

DEFINITION: one who opposes

Leslie was a constant **antagonist** to poor, sweet Egbert, always clawing at his soft underbelly and setting his hair on fire to delight the other kindergartners.

SYNONYMS: opponent, adversary
ANTONYMS: friend, ally

Notes Sometimes the word is used in a more narrow sense to mean "a villain in a work of fiction." The *antagonist* is the force that opposes the hero (or *protagonist*)—the Darth Vader to Luke Skywalker, for example.

The noun *antagonism* and verb *antagonize* are just as likely to show up on the SAT.

Assiduous [*adjective*]

DEFINITION: hardworking and persistent

Though I was **assiduous** and worked day and night to finish assembling this nuclear reactor, don't turn it on until I'm, oh, say 27.12 kilometers from the blast zone.

SYNONYMS: **diligent**, tireless
ANTONYMS: lazy, slothful

Notes The noun form is either the clunky *assiduousness* or the much more enjoyable *assiduity*.

Diligence [*noun*]

DEFINITION: perseverance, discipline

Although Veronica has the **diligence** of an A student, she prefers the hack-into-the-school-computer-and-change-your-grade method of study.

SYNONYMS: **assiduity**, industry
ANTONYMS: laziness, indolence

Notes You might also see the adjective form, *diligent*.

Asylum [*noun*]

DEFINITION: a place of safety or refuge

The United States refused to grant **asylum** to the refugees because, according to State Department officials, "They looked like fish, smelled like fish, and actually were fish."

SYNONYM: **sanctuary**, haven

Notes One common definition of *asylum* is "a hospital for the mentally ill," but this is a very narrow use.

An *asylum* can be a physical place, or it can be a condition of protection or safety, as when a country grants *political asylum* to refugees.

Sanctuary [*noun*]

DEFINITION: a place of refuge or safety

Thank heavens a **sanctuary** has been created to protect the world's least attractive mollusk, the poisonous, flesh-eating slime sucker.

SYNONYMS: haven, shelter

Notes See "Silence, Reticence" for notes on *sanctuary*. It's such a comforting word, we just had to use it twice. Now you have no excuse if you forget it on the day of your test, and no, you do not get your money back if you space out.

Adversity [*noun*]

DEFINITION: severe difficulty

It's amazing that with all the **adversity** police officers have to endure—shootouts, drug raids, car chases—they still find time to harass skateboarders.

SYNONYMS: misfortune, calamity
ANTONYMS: assistance, ease

Notes You'll often see the adjective form *adverse* describing anything difficult or challenging: "Although faced with unbelievably *adverse* conditions of rain, wind, waves, and giant killer squid, the Coast Guard managed to rescue the crew from a horribly slimy death."

If you remember that a related word, *adversary*, means "enemy" or "antagonist," the meaning of *adversity* isn't too much of a stretch to figure out.

Benevolent [*adjective*]

DEFINITION: kind and giving

Sister Mary Altruism, famous for her **benevolent** acts of kindness, was hailed as a national heroine for successfully smuggling blenders into smoothie-starved Wimponia.

SYNONYMS: **compassionate**, altruistic
ANTONYMS: selfish, malevolent

Deleterious [*adjective*]

DEFINITION: harmful or hurtful

Radiation has horribly **deleterious** effects on most living things, but if there's even a slight chance it can create a master race of mutant frog-men, I'm all for it. All hail the Frog-Men!

SYNONYMS: destructive, **injurious**
ANTONYMS: healing, helpful

Notes You won't often find the word *deleterious* used to modify anything other than "effects." It's most often used to describe health effects, such as the impact of pollution on living things (as in the above sentence). It often describes situations where the harmful effects aren't immediately apparent or happen slowly over time.

Enervating [*adjective*]

DEFINITION: exhausting

After 15 **enervating** minutes of trudging uphill, all I wanted was to flop on my couch, watch pro bowling, and scarf pork rinds.

SYNONYMS: arduous, fatiguing
ANTONYMS: energizing, empowering

Notes Many people confuse *enervating* with *energizing*, which is exactly the opposite. The ETS is betting you'll make the same error—don't do it!

The prefix, *e-* means "to remove" or "decrease" in Latin. *Nervus* means "muscles" in Latin. So, when you're *enervated*, your physical power decreases.

Exasperation [*noun*]

DEFINITION: extreme frustration or annoyance

Driven to the point of **exasperation** by a screaming baby in the theater, Daryl lost control and shouted, "Shut yer pie-hole, ya little freak!"

SYNONYMS: anger, aggravation
ANTONYM: calm

Hackneyed [*adjective*]

DEFINITION: lacking originality, overused

Get real! Do you really think I'd go for a guy who used a **hackneyed** old line like "Help, I'm drowning"?

SYNONYMS: **insipid, banal**
ANTONYMS: original, fresh

Jubilation [*noun*]

DEFINITION: extreme joy

Becky and William exploded in **jubilation** when their parents told them they were headed to Disney World, but their joy soon died when they learned they were really going to Lamp World.

SYNONYMS: **exultation, euphoria**
ANTONYMS: depression, sadness

Notes Other common forms are the adjective *jubilant* and the noun *jubilee*, which means "a celebration, especially an anniversary."

Sagacity [*noun*]

DEFINITION: keen judgment

Gilbert Worthington III was famous for his **sagacity** in making tough financial choices, but his accountants all agreed that buying a fast-food chain named PusBurger was not a wise decision.

SYNONYMS: perceptiveness, wisdom

ANTONYMS: obtuseness, stupidity

Notes Perhaps, dear reader, you've noticed that the prefix *sag-* is used in the word *sage*, meaning either "wise" or "wise person." You might also see the adjective form, *sagacious*: "It was indeed a *sagacious* decision to buy *Rock the SAT*, for without it, you might never have learned what *sagacity* means."

LYRIC FREAKS!

Directions: Fill in the blanks with a word (or words) from the lyrics.

1. Let me tell an anecdote, a funny tale
   About two people opposed in nature,
   _____.

   a. amicable
   b. benevolent
   c. incompatible
   d. inconsequential
   e. assiduous

2. Your love is _____, it's harmful
   and destructive

   Your love is _____, it makes me
   too tired to speak

   a. sagacious—incompatible
   b. diligent—frugal
   c. benevolent—a sanctuary
   d. deleterious—enervating
   e. exasperating—hackneyed

3. Lord give me sagacity
   Shine some _____ down on me

   a. wisdom
   b. kindness
   c. happiness
   d. comfort
   e. passion

4. I'm only looking for jubilation
   _____

   a. a short but overdue vacation
   b. freedom from your condemnation
   c. feeling every new sensation
   d. festive, joyful celebration
   e. a guide to help in pronunciation

5. I try to be _____
   Friendly, helpful, heaven-sent

   a. benevolent
   b. hackneyed
   c. assiduous
   d. frugal
   e. incompatible

PLUG IN!

Directions: Draw lines to match each word (or words) on the left to the correct definition on the right.

1. Anecdote
2. Incompatible
3. Inconsequential
4. Compassion
5. Amicable
6. Frugal
7. Camaraderie
8. Antagonist
9. Assiduous
10. Diligence
11. Asylum, Sanctuary
12. Adversity
13. Benevolent
14. Deleterious
15. Enervating
16. Exasperation
17. Hackneyed
18. Jubilation
19. Sagacity

a. Opposed in nature
b. One who opposes
c. Hard-working, careful, and attentive
d. Kind, generous
e. Irritation, frustration
f. Sympathy
g. Severe difficulty, misfortune
h. Extreme joy
i. Discipline, perseverance, hard work
j. Old, overused, lacking originality
k. Exhausting
l. Unimportant
m. Funny story
n. Friendship
o. Wisdom, keen judgment
p. Harmful, destructive
q. A place of safety or refuge
r. Friendly and agreeable
s. Cheap, stingy

AMP IT UP!

Directions: Fill in the blanks. Choosing the word (or words) that best completes the meaning of the sentence.

1. As roommates, William and Sally never got along; they were simply _____.

a. amicable
b. disastrous
c. incompatible
d. uninteresting
e. tiresome

2. In order to pass the final exam, you must work hard and remain _____. It would be a shame if all your _____ didn't pay off.

a. sagacious—misery
b. diligent—assiduity
c. benevolent—adversity
d. steady—frugality
e. amicable—camaraderie

3. This novel I'm reading is so trite and clichéd. It's a wonder any writer would dare publish such _____ work.

a. hackneyed
b. enervating
c. worthless
d. deleterious
e. inconsequential

4. Unfortunately for Shelly, her talent for grammar is _____, because it won't help her on the biology exam.

a. frugal
b. deleterious
c. amicable
d. inconsequential
e. adverse

5. After running 60 laps in almost record time, Alan collapsed on the bleachers, completely _____

a. diligent
b. jubilant
c. enervated
d. exasperated
e. benevolent

ANSWER KEY

Lyric Freaks!

1) c; 2) d; 3) a; 4) d; 5) a

Plug In!

1) m: 2) a; 3) l; 4) f; 5) r; 6) s; 7) n;
8) b; 9) c; 10) i; 11) q; 12) g; 13) d;
14) p; 15) k; 16) e; 17) j; 18) h; 19) o

Amp It Up!

1. c

In this case, choices b and e seem like they might fit, but they don't describe the relationship William and Sally have as precisely as choice c. If William and Sally never got along, they were *incompatible* (*About two people opposed in nature, incompatible*).

2. b

For this one, you need words with similar meanings for each blank. Knowing that alone, you can eliminate choices a, c, and d. Choice e is wrong because *amicability* has nothing to do with working hard. The words in choice b, however, *diligent* (*You laugh at my attempts, my hard work, my diligence*) and *assiduity* (*When I'm persistent, so hard-working, so assiduous*), mean exactly that.

3. a

Because you're looking for negative words, choices a, c, and e look tempting. How do you choose? Find the word closest in meaning to the keywords, *trite* and *clichéd*. If you know your vocabulary, it's not so bad, 'cuz that's exactly what *hackneyed* means (*It's getting old and hackneyed and it's making me so weak*).

4. d

If something isn't necessary or important in a given situation, like grammar on a biology exam, then it's *inconsequential* (*You think that I'm inconsequential, unimportant, just an orphan*). Choice e is wrong because it's not *adverse* to know grammar—that is, it can't actually hurt to know the grammar—but it won't help on the biology exam either.

5. c

There are a few possibilities here. Alan may have been *exasperated*, or even *jubilant* about running in record time, but nothing in the sentence tells us that for sure. The keyword *collapsed* most clearly indicates that he's *enervated*, or completely exhausted (*Your love is enervating, it makes me too tired to speak*).

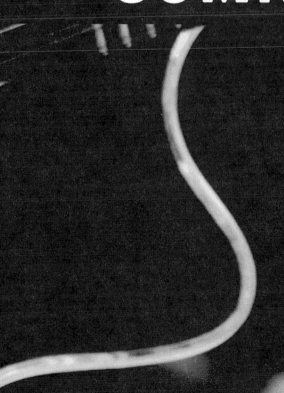

SOMNAMBULIST

Somnambulist

The results are **verifiable**
Yeah, you can prove it true
That I'm **incorrigible**
I can't be reformed—no, no, no

I **vanquish** all my enemies
I overpower them
Makes me feel **prominent**
A standout from the crowd, the crowd, the crowd

And I know I've been **recalcitrant**
Yeah I've been a stubborn one
Must be more **cognizant**
Aware of what's going on—on, what's going on

It's **ghastly** and it's frightful
And I wish I had a **sentinel**
A guard to watch my every move
And I've certainly had a **surfeit**
An excess of my problems
And I don't want no more of them

I've been such a **somnambulist**
Sleepwalking through this life
I've got to be more of a **hedonist**
Take pleasure from this life

The days tend to be a **labyrinth**
A complicated maze
I wait for the **zenith**
The high point of my days, my days, my days

The world's lost all its **vitality**
All of its liveliness
Makes me **abstemious**
Don't want nothing to eat or drink

My role's become **ambiguous**
It's **vague** and so unclear
What am I doing here
What am I doing here

It's **ghastly** and it's frightful
And I wish I had a **sentinel**
A guard to watch my every move
And I've certainly had a **surfeit**
An excess of my problems
And I don't want no more of them

I've been such a **somnambulist**
Sleepwalking through this life
I've got to be more of a **hedonist**
Take pleasure from this life

I need something beautiful
Appeal to me **aesthetically** (I've been such a **somnambulist**)
Something to **assuage** and soothe me
To **augment** and increase my intensity...

Verifiable [adjective]

DEFINITION: provable

Lucinda claimed to have **verifiable** proof that Bigfoot exists, but the authorities weren't convinced by the hairy stick figure she'd scrawled on a napkin.

SYNONYMS: authenticable, confirmable
ANTONYMS: unverifiable, unprovable

Notes This is the adjective form of *verify*, which hopefully you remember from "Imagination." The prefix *veri-* means "truth." (The motto of Harvard University is *Veritas*—Truth. And if you study with *Rock the SAT* long enough, you might just be wearing it on your sweatshirt). Thus, if something is *verifiable*, you can check its truth or accuracy.

Incorrigible [adjective]

DEFINITION: incapable of being corrected

Although Alphonso was an **incorrigible** bed wetter, he was able to lead a relatively normal life with the help of adult diapers and lots of bleach.

SYNONYMS: inveterate, hopeless
ANTONYMS: corrigible, reformable

Notes *Incorrigible* people are usually willfully resistant to change, or sometimes, as in Alphonso's case, just incapable of it.

The word derives from the Latin *corrigere*, "to correct." Hence, *correct* derives from the same root as *incorrigible*: a handy way to remember the meaning if you are an *incorrigible* forgetter of song lyrics.

Vanquish [verb]

DEFINITION: to conquer completely

Leslie **vanquished** Egbert on the kindergarten bus, easily overpowering him and harvesting his kidneys to sell on the Internet.

SYNONYMS: overpower, **subjugate**
ANTONYMS: surrender, submit

Notes *Vanquish* can mean to defeat an enemy, as in the sentence above, or it can mean to gain mastery over a problem or a difficult-to-control emotion: "Having *vanquished* her lust for fried ice cream, Lois was determined to get a handle on an even more overwhelming passion: butterscotch shrimp frittatas."

Prominent [adjective]

DEFINITION: easily recognizable, well-known

Ezra was easy to spot because of the **prominent**, unblinking third eye in the middle of his forehead.

SYNONYMS: outstanding, **conspicuous**
ANTONYMS: hidden, inconspicuous

Notes Remember *promontory* from the aptly titled song "Promontory"? It means "a ledge sticking out into space." Likewise, *prominent* describes anything sticking out noticeably.

You might see it in the case of someone who is well known in a particular field: "Though Dr. Hildegard Eckhardt-Schielenpfoff had achieved *prominence* in the field of linguistics, she was constantly embarrassed by her inability to say her own name without spitting."

Ghastly [*adjective*]

DEFINITION: terrifying or horrible

Even the most hardened policemen were forced to turn away from the **ghastly** sight of flames engulfing their beloved donut shop.

SYNONYMS: grotesque, gruesome
ANTONYMS: beautiful, pleasing

Notes Here's one of English's great underused words. It comes from the Old English word *gast*, meaning "ghost," or more generally any of the undead, like a walking skeleton, poltergeist (hear the similarity between *geist* and *gast*?), phantom, specter, apparition, vampire, and your garden-variety brain-eating zombie. So, anything *ghastly* is like a ghost—horrifying, frightening, or really gross.

Sentinel [*noun or adjective*]

DEFINITION: a guard

To ensure privacy, the teachers posted a **sentinel** outside the faculty lounge so that they could gossip about the weird-looking students.

SYNONYMS: sentry, watchman

Notes *Sentinel* will very rarely appear as an adjective to describe something watchful, as in a *sentinel* security camera.

The word derives from the Latin *sensus*, "to perceive," from which we get *sense*, *sensory*, and *sentient*. This last one means "conscious, aware," which is exactly what you want your *sentinels* to be.

Recalcitrant [*adjective*]

DEFINITION: disobedient, uncontrollable

Phyllis is as **recalcitrant** as a mule! She stubbornly refuses to play horsey even though I've promised to go easy with the whip.

SYNONYMS: stubborn, defiant
ANTONYMS: cooperative, obliging

Notes   This word has a cool derivation. It comes from Latin for the heel of the foot, *calx*. *Recalx* means "to kick back," which is why *recalcitrant* is often used to describe mules, which kick backwards when they're annoyed.

Cognizant [*adjective*]

DEFINITION: aware, comprehending

Because I'm **cognizant** of the fact that the albino dwarf hippo singing Motown in my shower *probably* doesn't exist, I think I'll go back to taking my meds.

SYNONYMS: informed, conscious
ANTONYMS: unaware, incognizant

Notes   This word shares a root with other words related to thinking and awareness, like *cogitate* (to think deeply—see "Spitball in the Eye"), *recognize* (become aware of again), *incognito* (hidden from awareness), and the noun form, *cognition* (awareness).

Labyrinth [*noun*]

DEFINITION: a maze

Lost in the city's **labyrinth** of streets and alleys, Alex gave up trying to find the art museum and settled into a park bench to scratch himself.

SYNONYMS: puzzle, tangle

Notes This word and its adjective, *labyrinthine,* come from an ancient Greek myth about Theseus, the hero who rescued a helpless maiden (is there any other kind in ancient myths?) from a maze called the *labyrinth.* The catch? At the center of the *labyrinth* was the Minotaur, a vicious beast with the head of a bull and the body of a man. Very imaginative, those Greeks. Also big on snake-haired women, sea-monsters, and flying horses. Must have been something in the water.

Zenith [*noun*]

DEFINITION: peak, highest point

At the **zenith** of her fame, Luscious T was the top star in the biz; the price she paid—selling her soul to the record company—was a bargain, since she didn't have a soul in the first place.

SYNONYMS: summit, pinnacle
ANTONYMS: nadir, low point

Surfeit [*noun or verb*]

DEFINITION: a surplus or overabundance

Thanks to satellite TV, we have a **surfeit** of channels. But do we really need IDN: The Icky Disease Network?

SYNONYMS: excess, **plethora**
ANTONYMS: scarcity, **paucity**

Notes Usually *surfeit* has a slightly negative connotation, as though there's an inappropriate excess, a glut of something. Although it sometimes appears as a verb to mean "feed" or "indulge," it's unlikely to appear in that form on your test.

Somnambulist [*noun*]

DEFINITION: a sleepwalker

Buckminster was more than a mere **somnambulist**; in his sleep he also cooked, fixed appliances, and scratched lewd portraits of Supreme Court justices on his Etch-a-Sketch.

Notes A 20-cent word, for sure, but it's easy to figure out when you break it down. *Somno-* is the prefix meaning "sleep," as in *somnolence*, or sleepiness. Combine it with *amble*, which means "to walk," and you've got *somnambulist* and its companion, *somnambulism*—the condition of sleepwalking.

Hedonist [*noun*]

DEFINITION: a pleasure-seeker

Being a **hedonist** isn't all fun and games, you know—actually, it *is* all fun and games; who's up for skinny-dippin'?

SYNONYM: sybarite
ANTONYM: ascetic

Notes Ever feel like you were born at the wrong time? The *Hedonists* were ancient Greek philosophers who suggested that the highest ethical good was something that gave pleasure to the senses. If it feels good, do it! They took their name after the Greek word for pleasure, *hedone*. Alas, *hedonism* didn't survive into our own time, which seems to be based on the opposite idea: no pain, no gain.

And, believe it or not, we even have a word for the inability to experience pleasure: *anhedonia*.

Vitality [*noun*]

DEFINITION: energy, health

Sure, taking up smoking will reduce your **vitality**, but think of all the joy you'll be bringing those poor little executives at the tobacco conglomerates.

SYNONYMS: heartiness, vigor
ANTONYMS: weakness, lethargy

Notes This is the noun form of *vital*, which means "full of life-energy." *Vita* is Latin for "life." *Vitality* can also be used to mean "endurance"—how long you can stay alive. It is also used to mean "lively" or "animated": "Javier was so full of *vitality*, cheerfulness, and life that most of us couldn't stand him for more than three minutes."

Abstemious [*adjective*]

DEFINITION: moderate, especially in eating and drinking

Although Martha was an **abstemious** drinker, we wanted her around at parties because she was not at all **abstemious** about sloppy, wet kisses.

SYNONYMS: temperate, reserved
ANTONYMS: immoderate, indulgent

Notes Know the word *abstain*, which means to "refrain from"? Well, *abstemious* has come to describe people who refrain from things. Especially fun things. The word originally related only to drinking booze; the root, *temetum,* is Latin for "strong drink." To be *abs-tem-ious* therefore originally meant to be moderate in drinking alcohol, but now it means to be moderate in general.

Ambiguous [adjective]

DEFINITION: not clear

When the space aliens said they'd like to have us for dinner, I found it pretty **ambiguous**. Either it was a sincere invitation, or we're gonna be mincemeat in an extraterrestrial sloppy joe.

SYNONYMS: **obscure, vague**
ANTONYMS: unambiguous, obvious

Notes *Ambiguous* can also describe something physically hard to see— "The shadowy, *ambiguous* shapes became clear in the moonlight, confirming candidate Blitzer's worst fears: the very Canadians he had vowed to enslave were coming to take him out."

Vague [adjective]

DEFINITION: unclear, difficult to perceive

Though we pressed him for details, Ottmar was understandably **vague** about how he came to be hog-tied in the girls' locker room.

SYNONYMS: **ambiguous,** indistinct
ANTONYMS: clear, distinct

Aesthetically [adverb]

DEFINITION: relating to beauty

Perhaps if your face were more **aesthetically** pleasing, I could tolerate your unbelievable stench.

SYNONYMS: beautifully, artistically

Notes *Aesthetics* is the branch of philosophy that examines the concept of beauty. *Aesthetics* tries to explain why most people find some things —like a rose or sunset—beautiful, yet we find other things—like a pile of trash or fat knees—not beautiful. An *aesthete* is a person who has a very refined sense of beauty in art.

Be careful not to confuse *aesthetic* with a very similar word, *ascetic*. An *ascetic* is a person who denies himself or herself pleasure or food, usually for spiritual reasons.

Aesthetic is sometimes spelled *esthetic*. Either way is correct.

Assuage [verb]

DEFINITION: to soothe or lessen

Some aspirin would **assuage** my pain, but it might also help if you quit punching me in the neck.

SYNONYMS: **mitigate, ameliorate**
ANTONYMS: aggravate, make worse

Notes *Assuage* can also mean "to pacify" or "quiet." So, if an angry mob shows up at your house demanding delicious candies, you might *assuage* their anger by handing out chocolate. Hey, it could happen.

It can also be used to mean "quench," as in *assuage* one's thirst.

Pronounce it *ass-WAJ* or *ass-WAGE*. We prefer the second one. The first is likely to get you soundly beaten up in an alley someday.

Augment [*verb*]

DEFINITION: to enlarge or add to

Seeking to **augment** his already considerable wealth, billionaire Gilbert Worthington III sold his cat to the local furrier for five bucks.

SYNONYMS: magnify, expand
ANTONYMS: reduce, lessen

Notes *Augment* can be used to mean both "increase in number" and "increase in size." If you have any trouble at all, remember the very common use of the word in our vain age of cosmetic surgery: the procedure called breast *augmentation*. Of course, this instance of *augment* means to "increase in size." It would be odd indeed if it meant "increase in number."

LYRIC FREAKS!

Directions: Fill in the blanks with a word (or words) from the lyrics.

1. It's _____ and it's frightful

a. incorrigible
b. verifiable
c. recalcitrant
d. ghastly
e. ambiguous

2. My role's become _____
It's _____ and so unclear

a. abstemious—prominent
b. somnambulist—vague
c. ambiguous—vague
d. recalcitrant—ghastly
e. incorrigible—prominent

3. The days tend to be a labyrinth
_____

a. A dreamy haze
b. A sleepy daze
c. A complicated maze
d. A self-destructive phase
e. An unstoppable craze

4. I've got to be more of a hedonist
_____ this life

a. Take pleasure from
b. Run away from
c. Make the most of
d. Gamble away
e. Find peace in

5. And I've certainly had a _____
An excess of my problems

a. labyrinth
b. surfeit
c. sentinel
d. zenith
e. somnambulist

PLUG IN!

Directions: Draw lines to match each words (or words) on the left to the correct definition on the right.

1	Verifiable	a. Pleasure-seeker
2	Incorrigible	b. Incapable of being reformed or corrected
3	Vanquish	c. Frightful, terrifying
4	Prominent	d. Outstanding, easily recognizable
5	Ghastly	e. Maze
6	Sentinel	f. Relating to beauty
7	Recalcitrant	g. High point, peak
8	Cognizant	h. Stubborn, disobedient, uncontrollable
9	Labyrinth	i. Provable
10	Zenith	j. Unclear
11	Surfeit	k. Sleepwalker
12	Somnambulist	l. Increase, add to or enlarge
13	Hedonist	m. Moderate, especially in food and drink
14	Vitality	n. Guard
15	Abstemious	o. Aware
16	Ambiguous, Vague	p. Soothe
17	Aesthetically	q. Excess, surplus
18	Assuage	r. Overpower, conquer
19	Augment	s. Liveliness, energy, health

AMP IT UP!

Directions: Fill in the blanks, using the word (or words) that best completes the meaning of the sentence.

1. We are fortunate to have one of the world's most _____ scientists on the university's faculty; her name is so recognizable, it brings instant credit to the institution.

    a. successful
    b. recalcitrant
    c. prominent
    d. cognizant
    e. ambiguous

2. Keeping watch, the _____ gazed into the distance beyond the castle walls. When he spied a horrifying and _____ horde of Mongol conquerors, he quickly roused the sleeping army.

    a. soldier–incorrigible
    b. somnambulist–vague
    c. sentinel–ghastly
    d. general–aesthetic
    e. hedonist–prominent

3. Upon waking to the sound of her alarm, Samantha became _____ that it was Friday, not Saturday morning, and she would have to get up for school.

    a. surprised
    b. cognizant
    c. inquisitive
    d. incorrigible
    e. vitalized

4. Because we already have a huge _____ of grain stored for the coming winter months, it is not necessary to _____ our food supply with rice.

    a. surplus–reduce
    b. silo–vanquish
    c. deficiency–augment
    d. surfeit–increase
    e. plethora–assuage

5. The results of the experiment were _____ and hard to understand; without _____ the results with further experiments, we will be unable to make any conclusions.

    a. ambiguous–augmenting
    b. incorrigible–utilizing
    c. vague–verifying
    d. useless–supporting
    e. recalcitrant–assuaging

ANSWER KEY

Lyric Freaks!

1) d; 2) c; 3) c; 4) a; 5) b

Plug In!

1) i; 2) b; 3) r; 4) d; 5) c; 6) n; 7) h;
8) o; 9) e; 10) g; 11) q; 12) k; 13) a;
14) s; 15) m; 16) j; 17) f; 18) p; 19) l

Amp It Up!

1. c

Choice a could be right, and so could choices b or d. What makes choice c the best answer? The fact that the scientist is well known. He may be *successful*, *recalcitrant*, or *cognizant*, but the keyword is *recognizable*, which suggests that he is *prominent* (*Makes me feel* prominent/A standout from the crowd...). This one looks easy, but it really ain't.

2. c

Choices a, c, and d all work pretty well for the first blank because a *soldier*, *sentinel*, or *general* could be keeping watch. But the keyword for the second blank is *horrifying*, and the only word that's synonymous with horrifying is *ghastly* (*It's* ghastly *and it's* frightful). Choice c is therefore correct.

3. b

We'd be surprised too if we thought it was Saturday only to find out it was Friday. But the reason *cognizant* is correct is because nothing in the sentence indicates that Samantha's surprised, so we can only assume the basics: that she's aware (*Must be more* cognizant/Aware *of what's going on...*).

4. d

Several choices work for the first blank because we're looking for a word that means "increase," but only two possible answers, choices c and d, fit the second blank. Choice c, however, doesn't work for the first blank because it would be necessary to increase the food supply if there was a huge *deficiency* of grain. Choice d works because *surfeit* means "surplus" (*And I've certainly had a* surfeit/An excess *of my problems*), and *increase* hits the nail on the head.

5. c

In science, the way to reach a conclusion is to verify, or check the accuracy of, your results (*The results are* verifiable/Yeah, you can prove it true). In this case, the author has to verify his results because the original experiment was hard to understand, or *vague* (*It's* vague *and so* unclear). The only other option is *ambiguous*, but *augmenting* the results with further experiments doesn't make as much sense as *verifying* the results with further experiments.

Team Rock the SAT

David Mendelsohn

Creator/executive producer/songwriter of *Rock the SAT*, also lead vocalist, guitarist, and coproducer on the *Rock the SAT* album. He earned his BA in music and English from Tufts University in 1991. David was a member, guitarist, and principal songwriter for Wind-up Records recording artist Trickside, which received significant airplay and attention in the United States as well as overseas. David has performed and toured around the country with Trickside, as well as with various bands around New York. He has also written music for and collaborated with other bands and performers, including 5NY. David was trained at the BMI Musical Theater workshop in Manhattan and has more than 15 years of songwriting experience.

Michael Moshan

Creator/executive producer/songwriter for *Rock the SAT*. Michael grew up on the killing streets of Dix Hills, Long Island. He earned his BA in Political Science from Washington University in St. Louis in 1991. After graduation, Michael played tennis professionally in France before earning a JD at the Benjamin N. Cardozo School of Law in 1995. Since then, Michael has written music and played keyboards with a number of New York-based bands, including the band Nonfiction. Michael continues to collaborate with some of the most exciting musicians in New York City while also practicing law as a real estate attorney. Michael currently lives in Williamsburg, Brooklyn.

Dr. Michael Shapiro

Chief editor/writer for *Rock the SAT*, Michael has been writing and teaching English and American literature, creative writing, composition, and journalism at the collegiate and secondary school levels for 10 years. He earned a BS in natural resources from Cornell University in 1990, an MA in English from the University of California, Davis, in 1992, and a Ph.D. in English and American literature from Brandeis University in 1998. Michael is currently Professor of English and Chair of the Department of English at TransPacific Hawaii College in Honolulu. He is an active writer; his works of poetry, fiction, and nonfiction, some of which have received awards, have been published in numerous journals and magazines. For many years, Michael has helped students succeed on the SAT verbal, both as a private tutor and classroom instructor.